The Seven Steps of Spiritual Intelligence

"The development of spiritual intelligence (SQ) is becoming mainstream and is a vastly personal journey that has rarely been taken. The SW 'Why?' question is also gradually becoming mainstream in an evolving knowledge economy. Most people even live life without asking why they are alive and what they should be doing. This book presents a fascinating and enlightening sequential framework in both exploring and developing SQ."
Dr. Stephen R. Covey, author *The 7 Habits of Highly Effective People* and *The 8th Habit: From Effectiveness to Greatness*

"The Seven Steps makes the development of spiritual intelligence accessible for all. It is at the leading edge and is vital for the individual and for the concerned professional. Read it!"
Stanley Rosenberg, expert in craniosacral therapy and Head of the Stanley Rosenberg Institute, Denmark

The Seven Steps of Spiritual Intelligence

The Practical Pursuit of Purpose, Success, and Happiness

Richard A. Bowell

NICHOLAS BREALEY
PUBLISHING

LONDON   BOSTON

First published in the USA
by Nicholas Brealey Publishing in 2005

3–5 Spafield Street
Clerkenwell, London
EC1R 4QB, UK
Tel: +44 (0)20 7239 0360
Fax: +44 (0)20 7239 0370

100 City Hall Plaza, Suite 501
Boston
MA 02108, USA
Tel: (888) BREALEY
Fax: (617) 523 3708

http://www.nbrealey-books.com
http://www.sq-training.com

First published in the UK by Nicholas Brealey Publishing in 2004

This book has been derived from and inspired by the philosophical writings and
researches of Leo Armin under the title of the "Template." The author is solely
responsible for the interpretation and concepts that derive from this work.

ISBN 1-85788-344-6

British Library Cataloguing in Publication Data
A catalogue record for this book is available from the
British Library.

Library of Congress Cataloging-in-Publication Data

Bowell, Richard A.
   The seven steps of spiritual intelligence : the practical pursuit of
purpose, success, and happiness / Richard A. Bowell.
      p. cm.
   Includes index.
   ISBN 1-85788-344-6
   1. Self-actualization (Psychology). 2. Multiple intelligences. I. Title.

BF637.S4B668 2004
158. 1--dc22

2004019752

Printed in the United States of America.

Contents

Preface

*We are not human beings having a spiritual experience. We are
spiritual beings having a human experience.*

Pierre Teilhard de Chardin

What is the meaning of life? What are we here to do?
Don't we all long to do something great in our lifetime and yet struggle to make sense of why we are
here? At our core we have a spiritual intelligence that is our
potential guide to the real meaning of the human experience,
why we are here, and what we are here to do. It is a pure light of
intelligence that illumines the way and nourishes all those who
long to live their lives meaningfully.

Our spiritual intelligence is the very foundation of self-
leadership. After all, how intelligent is it to be outwardly successful when we obscure this powerful core of intelligence and are
often stressed or depressed? How can we lead others from stress
and depression when they are struggling to find their own
meaning?

This book will take you on a journey through the seven
steps of releasing your spiritual intelligence, not by escaping from
the world but by engaging in it afresh with a new intelligence.
Through Steps One, Two, and Three—Awareness, Meaning,
and Evaluation—we become centered in our self and why we do
what we do (Step Four). This then enables us to take an overview
of the situation (Vision, Step Five), act with projection (Step Six),

and develop our effectiveness to realize our true mission (Step Seven).

Spiritual intelligence is not just about "what" we learn or "how" we behave, it is about "why" we do what we do. Unless we are developing our level of self, we are missing the most precious resource of all—our engagement in living.

Happiness, success, creativity, spontaneity, natural confidence, leadership—these are not things we can learn, not are they techniques or quick fixes that can be adopted. They are fundamental ways of engaging in a field of intelligence that is unlimited—spiritual intelligence.

Part I

Understanding Spiritual Intelligence

1

The Journey of the
Seven Steps

*Reality is a rich tapestry of interwoven levels, reaching from matter to
body to mind to soul to spirit.*

Ken Wilber

What you are about to read is an account of a journey, one that I have made and am still making. I trained in philosophy at university and have always had an interest in how our beliefs affect our lives. I believed from childhood that there is a purpose to human life and that there is a wise way to live it. I explored philosophy, major religions, and some new departures in thinking, but nothing seemed to fill my inner sense that I was looking for more than facts or information. My lost self was seeking to make a practical, feel-able, engaging journey.

This book distills a 16-year journey that I made into the field of spiritual intelligence into a map that I am now able to share with others with confidence and with good reasoning. I continue to spend my life refining and refocusing the best way to understand not merely what the journey is, but how to make it and why it is the most important journey anyone can undertake. But, as the saying goes, "the map is not the territory." Before we begin I want to trace the route ahead. I will stick to the metaphor of a journey so that when we come to the seven steps, it will be clear that each step is designed to take us along a particular path.

The landscapes ahead

The landscapes of the journey ahead are the rich fields of human intelligence. When we think about life, our jobs, our families, what we are doing, whether we are happy or not, we set out to answer these questions using whatever intelligence we have. The way we use intelligence inclines us to look for answers in certain places. For example, I may look for signs of happiness in my life in terms of material goods or satisfaction with my partner. If I dissect my life and decide that some parts of it don't make me happy, I can alter them. But what if happiness and all the important things I wish for are not visible to me in the landscape? What if I am searching for answers in a place where they don't exist?

Early in my own journey I was introduced to the idea that I was in the right place to find what I was looking for but had too little personal illumination to be able to see it. I was not aware in an illumined way. We are all too focused on finding an answer, a thing, a proof out there, and too little aware of the self that may shed light on what it is vital to see. The landscape of intelligence is more a state of affairs—as life is. Life is not one thing, it is feelings, thoughts, backgrounds, contexts, moments, and memories. It cannot all be reduced down to a patch of light in the brain where some activity is going on.

The vast landscape of intelligence can be seen through three distinct phases that together make visible the fields of intelligence: a childhood phase, an adolescent phase, and an adult phase.

When I was young, my childhood intelligence walked me through the world and I was filled with amazement and wonder. I kept on walking through the same world, but in time it began to seem less wonderful and became confusing, sometimes stressful, even worrying and frightening and not at all as happy as the childhood phase had been. When I checked with my childhood friends and others I met on the way who were then in their 30s, 40s, and 50s, I discovered it was the same for them. Even when they said they were admiring the landscape in their adolescent phase, they would often confess that underneath it wasn't so good.

If that were the end of the story and all we could do was make our house in the best place we could find in that somewhat disenchanted landscape, life would seem pretty miserable. But what if there were a further part to the journey where, if we kept walking, we would discover a new landscape, one in which everything that seemed gray and lacking in pleasure in fact gave new meaning to life? We can never go back to our childhood phase, but the adult phase of intelligence is childlike in its sense of meaning, light, interest, and engagement.

The third phase of intelligence is about finding the inner location from which our journey makes sense as a whole. Life is not a paradise lost but a paradise regained. Nevertheless, this phase cannot be reached by just continuing to walk on, hoping and wishing for better things. We actually have to stop the adolescent phase and deliberately choose to enter the adult phase.

The journey of this book will show how the three phases of intelligence are the meaning of our life—a state that I call "the truth of the situation." If we can understand the truth of the situation, we can begin to see that by taking steps to find new, uplifting, and inspiring things in the landscape everything changes. That is what the seven steps are there to help with: to walk through life and see richness and potential where before we may have been world-weary, despondent, and seeing nothing new.

Reframing intelligence

What does it mean to be intelligent? We must all have asked ourselves this question at some time in our life and felt how inadequate are the traditional guidelines that seek to address this issue. What we feel and sense ourselves to be is often so much more than those abilities that can be measured and graded in the available intelligence testing.

However, in the last 15 to 20 years, there has been a growing debate and some very substantive changes in how we think about the question of intelligence. Where once those who did not excel in examinations were considered to have "failed" in the system, we now have an open review of what it means to be intelligent in almost every field of life, an examination that is more concerned to discover human potential than to examine human failing. Perhaps, as many suspected, it is not we who have failed in the system, it is the system that has failed us.

This change is in no small part reflected in the astounding turnaround in brain science, psychology, and educational and learning theories. Gone are the days when the official line on intelligence was that it was a measurable quantity (IQ tests and SAT scores) and that everyone would find their place accordingly. It seems obvious now, but how could we ever have thought that our IQ, the level of which is largely set by the time we are teenagers, could be the ultimate measuring stick of our intelligence?

Since the early days of IQ testing, these measurements have served society's need to grade individuals for their fitness in work or for the military, their education, or their career. To evaluate everyone by this IQ way of thinking fails to recognize our multiple talents and, worse, instills an enduring sense of failure in those who do not conform to this narrow measurement as well as a false sense of success in those who achieve high scores. As we now know, both parties can feel distinctly unintelligent in the face of life's challenges and this is a feeling that it is very hard to shake off in later years.

In what has become something of a turning point in the dialog, Daniel Goleman's book *Emotional Intelligence* describes this change:

> *The brightest amongst us can founder on the shoals of unbridled passions and unruly impulses. People with high IQs can be stunningly poor pilots of their private lives. One of psychology's open secrets is the relative inability of college grades, IQ or SAT scores, despite their popular mystique, to predict unerringly who will succeed in personal life … At best IQ contributes 20% to the factors that determine success, which leaves 80% to other forces.*

Thanks in no small part to Goleman's book, the popularization of emotional intelligence—or EQ (short for emotional quotient), as I shall be calling it—has stretched the general framework of awareness about those "other forces" that may explain what it really means to be intelligent. Some of the factors that he identifies were once more likely to have been classed as traits or qualities of character:

❖ Being able to motivate oneself and persist in the face of frustrations.

❖ Being able to control one's impulses and delay gratification.

❖ Being able to regulate and monitor one's moods and keep distress from swamping the ability to think.

❖ Possessing the skill of empathy and the ability to hope for better things.

Goleman was able to draw on an impressive and growing body of brain science research to make the case that our emotions are an intelligence apart that is distinct and separate from our IQ, with its own wiring and capacity to illuminate action and, most importantly, with its own ability to learn and develop.

What we are yet to become

Nevertheless, this reframing of what it means to be intelligent to include emotional as well as cognitive abilities poses as many questions as it answers. Surely a complete model of intelligence must not only include the resources of what we know and who we are, but also what we are yet to become?

If intelligence is ultimately about the great potential of what we are yet to become, we must be bold enough to shift the paradigms of measurement from the IQ test to more existential qualities of our inner self and the deeper motives and reasons for us doing what we do. As we know, these are far less easy to quantify.

While we cannot yet talk of a measurable emotional or spiritual "quotient" in the same way as we talk of a level of measurable IQ, we can at least begin to talk openly in terms of an unlimited quotient of potential intelligence that we are yet to explore or become. This is the field of what we will be calling our SQ.

It is not a matter of engaging with an entirely new intelligence. We all have moments when we are creative, are compassionate, offer real leadership, and are deeply resourceful in bringing new solutions to the challenges we face. It is just that the focus and measurement of intelligence rarely acknowledge this higher kind of intelligence, let alone guide individuals to develop it.

The implications are enormous and far reaching. If we could more readily access this third kind of intelligence, might we not be able to bring our emotional responses and our reasoning to serve the same purposes rather than, as is frequently the case, being in conflict with each other? How often are we caught between head and heart, what it is good or right or effective to do, and the struggle to ensure that we have the character to act the part?

The Socratic maxim "know thyself," translated into today's terms, would marry the scientific discipline of understanding the workings of the brain (neuroscience) with the humanistic discipline of understanding ourselves and what we may yet become.

Integrating heart and head

Neuroscientist Joseph Le Doux raises the issue that some kind of integration or synthesis of heart and head, emotions and thinking (or even brain science and philosophy) might be the way ahead:

I conclude with the hypothesis, based on trends in brain evolution, that the struggle between thought and emotion may ultimately be resolved, not simply by the dominance of the neocortical cognitions over emotional systems, but by a more harmonious

integration of reason and passion in the brain, a development that
will allow future humans to better know their true feelings and to
use them more effectively in daily life.

How will this come about? Will this integration evolve over the course of time from the interaction of IQ and EQ, in the same way as two individuals who live together for a long time become more like each other or more able to live harmoniously (or at least learn to live with each other's failings more patiently)? Or is there a higher principle, another intelligence altogether, the presence of which enables thought and emotion to find a new harmony?

While I agree with Le Doux's premise, I will maintain in this book that the IQ and EQ model falls short of explaining the way in which this higher harmonizing process can develop. I want to show that what he calls "a more harmonious integration of reason and passion in the brain" is in fact the presence of a third distinct intelligence, spiritual intelligence or SQ. This is the intelligence by which we grow our level of self to integrate conflicts and become more than we are.

I also want to show that we can become aware of our SQ, that our ability to access SQ can be deliberately developed, and that this will in turn recruit IQ and EQ into a superior association. SQ is the life worth living, the happy life, the life of purpose that renews the marriage between our EQ and IQ within a new and meaningful context.

The heart (and head) of this book addresses exactly this: the challenge of breaking free from the confines that have been conditioned in us by the duality of our IQ and EQ and attuning ourselves to know this third and higher kind of intelligence that is so essential to our wellbeing and happiness.

There can be few greater challenges in the twenty-first century. This potential is not a remote genius in merely a few, it is an innate capability in everyone, and the application of this intelligence can apply to every moment of life. It is my task to make the case and show the way to remake a meaningful life, not by escaping from the world but by engaging in it afresh, with new intelligence.

Becoming meaningful

Let me begin by demonstrating the subtlety of this challenge with a simple exercise. Take a moment to register the words on the page in front of you, and then take a moment to register the fact that the words are also being registered on some inner screen, the primary visual cortex as it is called. The experience that we at first think of as being "out there" is also very much "in here."

However, what we call reading has a third aspect to it. It is not just information from the outside finding a way to become stored on the inside. It is more than mere process, a mix of emotional and mental. It is an event that is very much ours, it is happening in my case to me, to the "I" that I call my self or my sense of self. This "I" integrates the inner and outer worlds, the mental and emotional, and makes of the event a potentially meaningful experience that is unique. While two people can read a verse of Shakespeare and both catch the general meaning, with one person it may be a deeply revealing experience and with another it may seem artificial or contrite. The event is not general.

Anyone who has had to study and read extensively for exams knows the sense of sitting hour after hour taking in information and how different this is from the joy of reading for pleasure. Very much of our experience in this stressed and fast-moving world is of the uneventful, not-engaged kind. Our sense of self is often consumed in processing information, facts, low levels of emotional response, and mood changes, when such everyday experiences as reading, looking, talking, and working have the potential to be meaningful and rich.

This short exercise serves to illustrate the bind in which we are caught. We sense that we have lost the meaning of much of what we do, and yet we often feel helpless to stop doing what is meaningless. In fact, when stressed, our experience is that we do even more of what means less.

The meaningful level of self is when our self is engaged with a field of intelligence that brings new to the old and turns simple acts into events in which we are pleased to participate. This is spiritual intelligence and the SQ self is the level of individual self that engages with this field.

Such a level of self is more absent than it is present in life today. We variously shift from being smart to being dumb, from being emotional to being rational, from looking to the outside to looking to what we think is the inside—but what we sense is missing is the event of life itself. What we need to realize is that the purpose of life *is* to find the purpose of life—and then to live it.

An example from my own life will help illustrate what I mean. When I was 14, I found out that my mother was Jewish. I returned home from school one day and found my mother crying in the kitchen. My father was comforting her. This was unusual, since our family largely covered up our emotions. I was disturbed and later that evening, when my mother had gone to bed, I asked my father why she was upset. He explained to me how memories of the war had been evoked in her by her sister, an Auschwitz survivor, whom she had met in London that afternoon. They had lost their brother and both parents in the gas chambers.

I was thrown into turmoil, but realized that I had always felt a strange affinity for the Jewish children at school who took their morning services in a private room, while the rest of us, Protestants, gathered in the main assembly hall. I got every book I could out of the library about the war, the concentration camps, the plight of the Jewish people. I sat in my bed night after night looking at pictures of starving children in camps whose names I began to memorize and repeat to myself each day: Auschwitz, Birkenau, Treblinka, Buchenwald... I simply could not believe that such things could ever have happened and knew that they must never happen again.

I grew up and drifted into an identity that became immune to the horrors of the world, that could talk only glibly about making a difference, that had more important things to do than think about anyone else. What I then began to appreciate was that the fundamental issues that had been deeply awakened in me at 14 were the very same issues to which I returned 20 years later when I began actively to choose to "make a difference." I wept to think of how hard, how uncaring, how indifferent I had become, while feeling that this was exactly as it was meant to be.

The fact is that most of us are often blissfully unaware of why we do what we do. Though we may be well practiced at explaining or justifying our behavior in retrospect, we rarely consciously guide our actions toward a higher purpose from an evolving sense of self. In this one example, I saw something of the truth of my situation through these three distinct phases—my deep childhood knowing, my adolescent sense of being both lost and uncaring, and my adult reengagement that completed the truth of the situation.

Danish philosopher Kierkegaard once said: "Life can only be understood backwards; but it must be lived forwards." Perhaps spiritual intelligence can provide a way to resolve Kierkegaard's dilemma.

2

Being Spiritually Intelligent

The significant problems that we face cannot be solved at the same
level of thinking we were at when we created them.

Albert Einstein

The model of spiritual intelligence on which this book is based emphasizes three distinct process of intelligence: our traditional IQ, our emotional intelligence (EQ), and our spiritual intelligence (SQ). Let's take a brief look at IQ and EQ (there are many good books on these) and then a closer and deeper look at SQ.

For the moment let's simply identify IQ as the intelligence that seeks to understand the "what," EQ as the intelligence that seeks to understand the "how," and SQ as the intelligence that seeks to understand the "why" of things.

Each of these three intelligences has its own wiring in the brain (though with SQ recognition of this is a fairly new development in brain science), its own qualitatively different physiological experiences, and its own different facial expressions, which will be examined later in the book.

IQ

IQ is famously linear. Questions evoke answers in much the same way as neurons seek other neurons. One brain cell firing to another to form a neural tract is called synaptic transmission and is the basis for the formal logic of IQ. When we are asked a question—literally when someone fires a question at us—we usually are able to come up with an answer, hopefully the right or desired one. When the answer is slow in coming, we may well rub our chin or mutter to encourage the process.

Synaptic transmission is easy to test. If you are asked to name the capital cities of Europe or calculate 1/16th of 192, then you are likely to use your IQ wiring, which is ideally suited to reach into your memory to recall facts and make mathematical calculations. When you try it, you will notice that you are probably looking off to the side, trying to focus internally, as you might use the equivalent of a microscope to find some precise details, or outwardly, as you might when trying to find a book in a library. When the process is complete, you resume your "normal" gaze. It is largely mechanical.

EQ

EQ is different to IQ. It weaves associative patterns. A smell may evoke a memory that connects with the face of someone we love, then maybe to a time in Paris, to hopes and aspirations, longings and perhaps jolts of reality back to present responsibilities. It involves more of what we call our self.

Accessing our EQ is not like accessing an answer to a question or doing a mathematical calculation. Imagine you are introduced to a friend's acquaintance with the words: "I am sure you two will have a lot to discuss, you have so much in common." No amount of IQ will create the empathy and rapport needed to discover the sense of having things in common with another person, as this is an emotionally based intelligence process. Rapport and empathy are not merely a matter of similarity of facts or interests, but they are the note and tone of *how* we process those interests and *how* they can harmonize between any number of people.

In a meeting where everyone pursues the same interest, be it a football supporters' club or a Wagner appreciation society, that note and tone are present even before any word is spoken or any overture played. This is a key element in team building and empathy, as it is in any relationship.

Emotional intelligence is not accessed like a fact or an answer, it is more a process of scanning the ways we have experienced things working in the past and anticipating the ways we might operate in a new situation, seeking and measuring appropriateness to the context of "new friend" or "lover of Wagner" or whatever it may be. Context, memory, comparison, appropriateness—these are EQ skills.

We develop "templates" of experience that we apply within different contexts: new friend, ex-wife, potential business partner, mother to our children, and so on (perhaps even all of these at once!). In his famous book *The 7 Habits of Highly Effective People*, Stephen Covey calls these attributes "character." The "character ethic," as he refers to it, considers the needs of others and of society at large and works toward there being a better level of value, association, and harmony.

In this EQ process, we may notice that we become expressive, particularly in the middle part of the face, muscles lifting in a smile or held taut in an attitude of hesitation or doubt. Our body language could be termed "experimental personal theater," designed to tune into our likes, dislikes, and values and compare them to what we sense are the other person's. It is like a very advanced version of two dogs sniffing each other (no accident that the emotional brain is also called the rhinencephalon or "nose" brain).

SQ

When we come to consider SQ, no amount of scanning or searching within will find the answer to such questions as "how" to be happy, "how" to be successful, "how" to find inner well-being, "how" to become more creative, "how" to be a good leader or a good father or mother. In fact, these are not even "how" questions, they are "why" questions. "Why do you want to be a good leader, father, mother?" is an original question that is unmediated by previous experience. We have made it a "how" question in the absence of our third, searching intelligence.

This is not a "how" book. It is a book that explores the core *reasons* for doing what we do. This is different to the way we have become accustomed to using "why," which is mostly to suggest that when we get the answer we will be able to move on and do something.

"Why" is a process of engaging our self with the unlimited fields of intelligence that we call SQ. It develops a sense of self that is not the result of ideas or views or opinions or experiences. It is beyond character—it is the natural genius of living that everyone is heir to. This process can become a state of living in awe and wonder, interest and enthusiasm, where new levels and new insights are the signs of becoming more "why-fully" engaged as new intelligence is able to flow.

This is what makes it difficult to co-relate specific brain activity with SQ, though there has been a notable success in this area. These early observations show how the brain exhibits moments when the whole cortex becomes aroused as a singular coordinated event. Notice the difficulty of language: I say "how" the brain...

Neuroscientists speak about the "what" and the "how" pathways, but the "why" pathways are not etched in our brain in the same way. It is quite understandable that the most up-to-date brain scanning equipment is focused on a "what" in some locality of the brain or on a "how" as one brain lobe interacts with another. The "why" is a presence generated afresh each time and is not measurable in the brain as a local area of activity or a function of one part associating with another. The best we seem to be able to do is witness moments of inexplicable wholeness.

Where most progress has been made in measuring SQ has been in the fascinating accounts of the brain activity of high performers, meditators, and athletes, where it is their overall state or presence that is of paramount importance. Combinations of high intensity and low blood flow, great focus, and yet extremely relaxed heart rate—these are the early indications that the brain does have an overall presence or sense of function.

These observations are both puzzling and profoundly significant, given science's historical preoccupation with finding some central controlling intelligence in the brain mass. Here at least, neuroscience has shifted its focus from brain malfunction to brain super-function.

My own belief is that the overall functioning of the brain is directed from a higher level of intelligence, a presence of self that is generated by exploring the fields of the unknown that cannot yet be measured directly by equipment that is "what" or "how" based.

Climbing the mountain

The experience of this SQ engagement requires a third kind of expression as a process that marries inside and out, emotional and cognitive, known with newly coming to be known. It can be likened to climbing a mountain and, after hours of hard struggle, turning to face out from the mountain and take in the view. The sense of the moment might carry an underlying emotional satisfaction, an IQ calculation of how high we have climbed and how long it has taken to reach this point—and yet there is more. The act of looking out constitutes a new level from which things are identifiable—"look, there's the house we are staying in, there's the church"—but at the same time different and new. It causes us to review all we had previously thought was the case in a new light and from a new perspective.

SQ is the culminating presence of the mountain in the person and the person on the mountain—hard to explain in language. We are still and quiet inside but what we see is intense and fresh. We are not looking at the details outside from some inner screen inside; we are aware of the whole scene below from an inner presence that is also whole. Perhaps we are drawn to the nature of the town, the sense of life going on, and the patterns of people and activities. Maybe we find ourselves wondering how this town came to be, what caused it, the lives that have come and gone, and the state of the town as it is today in its own unfolding story. Within these observations we would have a very exact sense of self within the event.

Such engagement in just the event of looking is possible in daily life. Conversation, ordinary work tasks, even argument and conflict can all be endowed with a sense that we are engaged afresh and anew, in which we review all our previous thoughts and experiences (EQ and IQ) within a new context.

In a similar way, I have heard from many skilled skiers that when they really ski well it is the mountain that is guiding the person and the person and the mountain become a unified experience. When she won the Olympic Gold medal, champion skier Diane Roffe-Steinrotter said: "I felt like a waterfall." Was she describing herself or the mountain? Both, it seems to me.

Self-leadership

Given the acute scanning faculties the human brain possesses (it can read minute cues of impending danger or someone's genetic code in a faint smell that we are not even consciously aware of), developing the ability to "read" the finer and deeper causes of things is a potential gift in any situation. Whether it is listening to a child, a partner, or a client, being able to pick up on the subtle cues that this more intelligent level of self passes to others enables us to understand deeply what the other person is saying, "where they are coming from."

SQ is first and foremost self-leadership. By listening or talking in an SQ-seeking way, we are choosing to develop that unique presence of our self in its engagement with the bigger picture and the subtle cues from this more intelligent level of self pass to others. There is no need to attach our customary sense of self-importance to what we say to influence other people in favor of our views or decisions.

SQ is the pure light of intelligence—it is illuminating and others pick up on it and want to feed on it. It nourishes, to paraphrase a well-known beer advert, the parts that other intelligences can't reach.

To get first-hand experience of this, try listening to a symphony like Beethoven's marvellous 9th and wonder how a composer could create such a sense of overall integration by writing a symphony laterally, note after note. Resist the emotional draw of getting lost in the melody and try to listen to the whole.

Clearly, Beethoven had the entire symphony in his head all at once. He could "see" his music in his head, just as Einstein could see mathematical formulae.

Those who are engaged in spiritual intelligence processes cannot easily convey to those who do not have the experience just what it is like to be up on the mountain. Those innermost and meaningful experiences that we have as individuals are not easily translatable into explanation or emotion (IQ and EQ). And here we come to a conundrum about a book on SQ: It cannot be accessed by an explanation and it cannot be engaged through our emotions. It needs us somehow to recognize it, affirm it, awaken it, and perceive it by resisting the usual ways of making our journey through life.

3

Understanding the Truth of the Situation

He who has a why to live for can bear almost any how.
Friedrich Nietzsche

A t any moment we are acting and living within some context or situation or another that we call our life. We may be at work, lying on a beach, stuck in a traffic jam—during the course of the day we move through many acts of a play. In each we have a broad range of emotional reactions. Some are juvenile, some irresponsible, some considered. We may love or hate work, put up with it or relish its challenges, long to be at the beach or out of this damn traffic jam. Quite naturally, we try to minimize the bad experiences and amplify the good.

Consider for a moment the question:

What do you understand is the truth of your own situation
at this very moment?

Put down the book and resist reading on until you have given yourself some minutes to contemplate your answer.

You will have likely considered some of the following features relating to the truth of the situation:

❖ The immediate environment you are in.
❖ Your age.
❖ Your career.
❖ Whether you have a family.
❖ Where you live.
❖ Your mood.
❖ What happened today, maybe an argument or a good moment with a friend.
❖ How you feel, whether or not you are happy, sad, fulfilled, unfulfilled.
❖ Whether you have goals, purposes, targets, visions.
❖ Whether you feel good about how well you are doing with regard to how you would want your life to be.

Of course, all of these are part of life but may seem like so many fragments without some unifying context. Many elements of the situation may conflict with others: I still feel young even though I am close to 60—I want to do more but my commitments don't allow me to—If I wasn't surrounded by this team the whole project would be flying by now—If I didn't have financial commitments I would have left.

The SQ way of thinking starts by exploring the larger context of life as primarily important, rather than finding meaning in arranging the details. It says that no matter what we are doing, there is at that moment a main theme underpinning all of our experience.

Once we understand the truth of that theme, there can begin to be continuity and meaning to the whole of life as we live it. We cease to be subject to the emotional attachments to each small act; instead, we develop an inner freedom that opens up all kinds of opportunities to act and be intelligent in the present that otherwise would not be accessible.

I remember being in a traffic jam with the man to whom this book is dedicated, Leo Armin. I was clearly wound up, tense, utterly focused on getting to our destination, and frustrated at not being able to move a single meter forward, when he turned to me and said quietly: "This is still our time. This is still our life." In that moment my awareness shifted from the frustrations of the traffic jam to the challenge to engage. The car, the other person, and I were all that was in the now—in that moment he nudged me toward the why that caused me to engage with what was present. I felt how immature it was of me to keep projecting my energies toward a place that I knew I would be frustrated in getting to. No matter how hot I became, I was not going to change the fact that I was stuck.

I call this greater context of life the truth of our situation. This book focuses on the intelligence that understands the truth within each and every situation. More than possessing a high IQ or a mature EQ, understanding the truth of our situation at any moment is the most intelligent and practical pursuit. When we understand why things are the way they are, we are able to engage wisely and maturely. SQ brings maturity to EQ and IQ.

The three levels of truth

So, what is it to understand the truth of the situation? Our first insight might be that each situation is different and therefore the truth of each situation must be different. Truth exists at each level of the great chain of being. What we perceive as the truth of our situation is as much to do with what intelligence perceives it to be. To ask about the truth is one thing, to seek the truth another, but to knock on its door, to face the truth in ourselves, is something quite different. Sometimes we find that the door is right in front of us and is opened inwardly not by pushing harder but by trying less in the wrong way with the wrong intelligence.

Truth one: Temporary truth

Temporary truth is what we call truth today that proves itself not to be true tomorrow or in the next moment. Temporary truth is nothing more than the ephemeral way we color each changing moment or each changing moment colors us. We balance one material reality with another. When we are based in temporary truth we are mostly aware in an alarmist way, too personal, too changing and reactive, trying to center ourselves in a state that makes us feel good or provides (temporary) relief from stress or effectively avoids the greater truth of our situation. Temporary truth is the domain of the fixed intelligent identity that imprisons our SQ core.

To adhere rigidly to temporary truth is the identity of the lost, the avoider, the shallow, and the superficial. As long as we are in the grip of the temporary truth we will never see from the new intelligence at our core.

I am driving my car along a country road one morning, telling myself that everyone on the road should drive slowly so they can take in the sights and sounds and sensations along the way. I mentally pass this as a law, a decree that everyone should obey, having seen the merit of it personally. It is safe, considerate, and makes perfect sense to me as I lightly touch the button that winds down the window and let the spring breeze gently waft through the car to the exact degree that is comfortable.

I am driving at 50 kph and enjoying the views and the sun and I don't want to be pressed by anyone. Life is good with my new law that all drivers should drive slowly and considerately. I won't have my world disturbed by those who do not adhere to the law of the road as I have passed it.

I become aware of a car behind me that is contravening this new law. It wants to overtake. I am doing 50 kph in a 50 kph zone, so my law also conforms to the traffic regulations on this road. I am vindicated and proved right once again. I have a legal right to resent the person behind me exerting pressure on me to go faster (as it seems).

My awareness is firmly shaped by the temporary truth I have adopted. The potential for rage is lurking under the bonnet and I am ready to explode at those who might disturb the peace.

However, I am suddenly jolted into another perception as I notice the time. I didn't realize I had spent so long getting to this appointment. I haven't got all day just to admire the view, I have work to do. Another temporary truth supplants the previous one, equally compelling and "right" as the previous one, and I put my foot down, 50, 60, 70 kph. No one drives within the speed limit, I tell myself. Limits are just indications to sensible people.

A new philosophy emerges. Everyone should drive efficiently to get where they want. Driving is not something that should be sightseeing on wheels. If you want to enjoy the view, get out and walk, don't hold everyone up.

My temporary truth has shifted to another temporary truth. The slow driver in front of me, who a moment before I had seen as my buddy, suddenly becomes my mortal foe, holding me up and preventing me from getting to my appointment. As I overtake, my suspicions are confirmed—the driver even looks selfish and mean.

The more fixed and intolerant we are in ourselves, the fewer the range of choices we perceive. To put it in biological terms, the more we use ourselves up in altering the temporary truth, the more we diminish the resources of our immune system, the less we can tolerate any flux that allows real change. Good and strong immunity provides the basis for broad-based elective behavior.

Truth two: Semipermanent truth

Semipermanent truth encompasses the daily rules and parameters that life defines. The rules of a football match, social conventions, agreements to be on time, politeness, courtesy, decency, the rules of engagement between the collective of society and the individual— these are the domains of semipermanent truth, without which life would be disordered and intolerable. They are laws of convention, albeit ones that can be stretched this way and that. They are socially evolved from our history—they make sense even if they are at times interpreted to the advantage of the self-centered.

What would it be like to play a sport like golf, football, or baseball without any rules? The process of the game would be quite aggravating, meaningless, and without pleasure. We may try to get away with stretching the rules, but we don't want to be seen as out-and-out cheats. It is precisely within the rules of engagement that the merit of the sport is discovered, just as it is within the rules of daily living that we derive notions of success. Even being good losers has its virtue (at least for the British!).

The contest, the act of self-proving, the search for excellence, winning "fairly," developing skills, extending the physical and mental limits—these would be lost if there were no rules by which to measure the effort taken.

27

Semipermanent truths enshrine our fight or flight ethic. We want to win and we want to ensure that we don't lose, so we evolve rules that give parameters of behavior ensuring that the spoils of battle are as evenly divided as they can be regulated to be.

If we are watching a football match and winning is everything for us, what is important will be perceived accordingly. Our awareness will not be of the whole match but more of the performance of our team in relation to scoring goals. It is the struggle not to lose, the drive to win, the competition itself that spur the team and the individual to try to excel. This is the fight and flight competitive edge.

My wife and I wanted to sell our house and went to a local real estate agent. He came to look at the house and suggest a price. He would sell the house more quickly if the price were low, but if he set too low a price he knew that we would go to another agent and he would make no commission. So the two considerations lean in different directions and define the convention. He would make the seller happiest if he sold the house at a high price and he would make the buyer want to buy the house if the price were kept low.

However, a "fair price" that a real estate agent comes to because he knows he can't get away with cheating either the buyer or the seller is not the same "fair price" as that to which someone comes from the notion of fairness as a first principle, even though both processes may arrive at the same price.

Semipermanent truth is the domain of character, what is decent and legitimate, what observes the "rules of engagement" that maintain fair standards and decency. It suggests an individual who has reached their own views and is reliable, trustworthy, and sincere. They make a profit but acknowledge that it is their hard work, their reliability that is being paid for. Character must always have recourse to a higher domain of self-questioning, otherwise it is nothing more than an outward act. This domain is the consideration of permanent truth.

Truth three: Permanent truth

Permanent truth is always the greater truth, the higher truth, the level of truth that we cannot escape, manipulate, cheat, or get away from. It is this truth that I call the truth of the situation.

We can only acquiesce to permanent truth and understand its influence, we cannot manipulate it for our own ends. It is a law in the way that Cecil B. de Mille describes in the film *The Ten Commandments*: "It is impossible for us to break the law. We can only break ourselves against the law."

The laws or principles of permanent truth describe the "why" of the bigger picture. Plant a tree and watch it grow every day through the four seasons and you will know beyond a shadow of a doubt that there is intelligence in the growth of all things. Nevertheless, a flower growing or a season passing represents the childhood expression of the law. They do not have a choice.

What makes the human part in intelligence so compelling is that we can deliberately embrace whatever level of truth we choose. If we return to the three stages of intelligence, we can see how and why this principle governs the potential process of human growth.

We are born with an SQ core that is fully engaged and in time that "season" passes. In place of the inner driving SQ core, we become aware of a space that invites us to step in, to choose, to become. This is a different kind of engagement than childhood. If we do not choose to engage in that opportunity, childhood will forever remain the high point of our life and all the rest will carry a sense of diminishment or failure. We will remain in adolescence for life. Even the feelings of existential emptiness that we ascribe to depression, anxiety, or burnout are meaningful in that they bring to our awareness an increasing consciousness of the choice to live that we have not yet made.

The SQ path is a life that examines the truth of the situation, that leaves nothing to chance, that wishes to join the truth of the situation at the highest level and is a level of self based in permanent truth. It is more than character: it is the core of meaning based on core principles. It cannot be approached as a secondary element—it is the first principle of every adult life.

Permanent truth was there before we arrived and will be there after we leave. For example, I am willing to bet everything I own that the sun will rise tomorrow. Let me explain.

Everyone has watched the sun rise at some time. The event can play out in many different ways, depending on the level of truth that the self is dwelling in:

❖ Did you know that the light from that great ball of fire takes more than 11 minutes to arrive at this planet at a speed of 150,000 km a second—awesome, isn't it?

❖ It's just so beautiful, so wonderful.

❖ Did I tell you about the time I saw the sun rise when I was in the Arizona desert?

Each of these combines elements of temporary or semi-permanent truth.

The SQ-centered individual looks at the sun rise from their permanent SQ core. As they observe the permanent truth of the scene, they will be drawn more to observation of the incredible mechanics of it, the way permanent truth repeats itself through exact laws, in the order of each day, in processes such as the seasons passing, in getting older, being born, and dying.

The event of the sun rising will evoke feelings (not emotions) of mortality and it will quicken in the individual the desire to do something important, enduring, and meaningful with their life. I say these are feelings rather than emotions because feelings are always SQ influenced—they are always endowed with meaning from the core and, most importantly, they provide a sense that the greater truth is meaningful and safe to enter.

Dwelling on permanent truth, even for 15 minutes a day, can inform the brain that this is the context through which you choose to view the world. After all, dwelling on the car or dress you want to buy will inform the reticular formation and the hippocampus (believed to handle the context of our awareness) that this is important and your brain will notice examples of that car or that dress at odd moments throughout the day. Using the same principle to provide a context for greater truth is to fashion a context in which to better understand the truth of the situation.

The great chain of being

Our education and our culture mostly foster a greater interest in temporary and semipermanent truth than in permanent truth. American philosopher Ken Wilber describes how our present culture seems almost to encourage a broken and incomplete sense of self.

> *The modern West, after the enlightenment, became the first major civilization in the history of humanity to deny almost entirely the existence of the Great Nest (or chain) of Being. In its place was a "flatland" conception of the universe as composed basically of*

matter (or matter/energy) and this material universe … could be
studied by science and science alone.

The great nest or chain of being that Wilber describes is not only the interconnectedness of the world that we view outside ourselves, but the evolving inner event that views the world—our evolving self. Any theory of consciousness needs to recognize that the self that views the world is also a chain of being that has itself become broken (in its adolescence) and must be made whole (in a new adulthood). All the wisdom traditions in history recognized this great chain of being as the core of life. The examples I gave of the three levels of truth show that both the outer and inner worlds have been ruptured.

Wilber describes the great chain of being as having three "eyes of knowing":

❖　　The flesh (empiricism).
❖　　The eye of mind (rationalism).
❖　　The eye of contemplation (mysticism).

The Hindu and Buddhist notion of these three states encompasses the gross level (body and matter), the subtle level (mind and soul), and the causal level (spirit). As we elevate from level to level, we also discover new and more subtle faculties that the baser levels do not contain.

I prefer the following description:

❖　　Temporary truth—the domain of materialization or end results (IQ).
❖　　Semipermanent truth—the domain of process (EQ).
❖　　Permanent truth—the domain of origination (SQ).

We live in an age that almost exclusively eyes the world through the material reality and/or the rational eye of the mind. Little credence is given to the "spiritual," even though new paradigms speak extensively of the soul and the spirit. The way that spirituality is incorporated (made into body) in the lower levels always confines the spiritual to an add-on feature of the material universe. Spiritual intelligence is the innermost quality, the presence, the emanation, the mystical, the higher, the origination, the virtual domain, which exists before process enfolds it with mind and matter. It is the level that we can only aspire to, we can never possess or violate.

4

Growing: The Three Phases

An unexamined life is not worth living.

Socrates

W e tend to think of intelligence as a uniquely human property and begrudgingly accord other forms of life the title of being "less intelligent." This kind of overly personal attachment prevents us seeing just how intelligent life itself is.

To understand the intelligence potential of a life, I propose to look at the three obvious phases through which each life journeys: childhood, adolescence, and adulthood. I shall explore the way intelligence grows, structures, and restructures itself in these "organizational changes." To be aware of these phases, which are universal in that every life passes through them, at least to some degree, is to understand the truth of the situation and to live in the potential that each phase offers.

The idea that we have just one monolithic kind of intelligence that endures all of our life and peaks around the end of adolescence is happily out of date, although our thinking very often still reflects. Inside each of us there are many strands of intelligence—IQ, EQ, and SQ—and they are not all living in harmony, neither are they all at the same age or level of maturity.

34

The phases of life are arranged purposefully and meaningfully and only SQ can attune itself to know this.

Phase One: From birth to adolescence

As you might have guessed, understanding the truth of the situation does not mean using our EQ and IQ to answer a question or reevoke our experience of life. To understand the truth of our situation is to understand the permanent, unchanging context of life itself, which is an expression of the higher fields of intelligence. The truth of these higher levels is always unfolding, revealing, making itself known. We have at our core a spiritual intelligence that, if liberated, would be discovering why we are here, what we are here to do, and how to do it all of the time.

Figure 1 shows the three intelligences as they are at birth and in our childhood years.

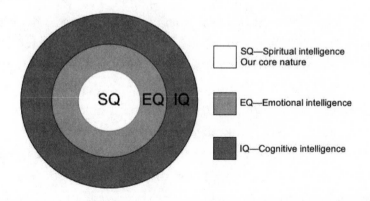

Figure 1

The experience of childhood is of a core inquiring spiritual intelligence that seeks to know and to explore the world. It is a time when our driving interest in the world engages all of our intelligence systems, IQ, EQ, and SQ. They are active and in full and vigorous growth and working in harmony. We naturally live in the moment and that moment unifies and binds our experience together—there is an unseen context that makes a wholeness of life. We are at one with the world.

I can remember this feeling so well. It is early spring and I am sitting at my desk at school. It is Latin class. We are seated alphabetically and it is my good fortune (the only good fortune of my name) that the "Bs" have window seats.

From there, I can look out on the school gardens and a small wood. On this particular morning the sun is shining brightly and my awareness is gripped by a very large bumble bee nestling into a flower just outside the window. Even now I can see it sipping the nectar, dancing from bloom to bloom. I don't know how long I have been looking, I only know I am in the moment and I want to be nowhere else.

I was engaged in a field of intelligence from which I came to know so much. A child's preoccupation with "what" something is is expressed by them simultaneously trying to discover "how" it works with an intensity and curiosity about "why" the world is the way it is.

Years later, I discovered that what my intelligence systems knew in those precious moments that I stole from learning Latin was indeed highly accurate and meaningful. Today, I would say that this was an SQ moment in which my EQ and IQ were entirely in accord. I later discovered in a book by zoologist John Downer that the bee I had been watching was a better medium of tuition than my Latin teacher could ever have hoped to be:

Bees are highly sensitive to electrical charges. A bee's whole body is negatively charged. This fact has been exploited by flowers

whose positively charged pollen is able to leap on any visiting bee
thanks to the forces of opposites attracting.

Opposites attract. I was being introduced to a great law of life that I later learnt with my IQ in physics class some time later, but not so eloquently. I use this as an example of all three intelligences working in harmony. We know with our SQ what our EQ feels and our IQ remembers the facts and the interchange between them, sifting through the experience in a harmonious dialog that may prevail for a lifetime, continually revealing new insights.

Understanding the law or principle rather than learning the answer to a question becomes vital in engaging in the truth of any situation. The poignancy of the experience of watching the bee was that through it I became engaged with some realm of intelligence, so different to learning Latin verbs by rote.

In later life I was able to apply the principle that opposites attract usefully in many situations. I observed that behavior can be "negatively or positively charged" to attract some things and not others, I deliberately applied the same principle in understanding situations of conflict, and I also like to think that it had a hand in my wife and I coming to be partners.

In those early years our deepest nature is engaged with the world and this engagement forms our deepest nature. While in this first phase we may not be aware of our search from a detached perspective, we most definitely *are* the search in the way we embody that core intelligence.

If you try to recall those things that caught your awareness in childhood, they will be deeply expressive of your core nature as it was formed in those early years. This comes to play a meaningful and significant part in what each one of us does in our later life and mission, and for each person it is different.

Phase Two: Adolescence

At the onset of adolescence the driving power of the SQ core that characterizes our childhood years begins to retreat and the natural harmonies of childhood give way to a time of turbulence and an increasing inner sense of emptiness and unknowing.

In Figure 2 we see that the SQ core is weaker and less compelling and gives way to an inner space that is the promise of a whole new intelligence potential—the development of self.

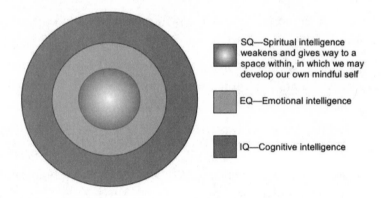

SQ—Spiritual intelligence weakens and gives way to a space within, in which we may develop our own mindful self

EQ—Emotional intelligence

IQ—Cognitive intelligence

Figure 2

At first, this change causes imbalance in the emotions that have been used to being led by natural interest and enthusiasm about the world. Teenagers can be pretty unreasonable too!

Adolescence is a second life. It requires a new kind of intelligent approach. We are no longer innocent because we consider our motives and actions, and yet we mostly do not yet know what are the right ways to. We are yet to build our own self with a mind that can guide us wisely.

It is a time filled with uncertainty and the development of character—very much what we today call emotional intelligence or EQ—has the direct function of keeping the opportunity of future growth and development open by virtue of clear values and standards. Character building needs to begin in childhood to ensure that this second phase does not cause shock and retreat from the great opportunity of adolescence.

In childhood we are minded (looked after) by our parents. Now we need to develop our own mind and often find this immensely difficult with our IQ-biased education. The main function of character is to sustain us in the change from childhood to adolescence and future adulthood, and now it is easier to see why the attributes that we mentioned before as EQ developments are so vital:

❖ Being able to motivate ourselves and persist in the face of frustrations.
❖ Being able to control our impulses and delay gratification.
❖ Being able to regulate and monitor our moods and keep distress from swamping our ability to think.
❖ Possessing the skill of empathy and the ability to hope for better things.

These are all value forming and all inform our deeper core that this is a journey phase of search and exploration. They allow us to shift successfully from childhood to adulthood by exploring what we may become.

As we know, this phase can be a radical and even shocking change. It is no less startling than if my cat suddenly became aware of itself and wondered what it was doing on the sideboard with a mouse in its mouth. If it could, it would ask: "Why am I here? Who put me in the driving seat?" It would no doubt consider my look of disgust and wonder if it was OK to have a half-dead mouse in its mouth. It would begin to question itself and wonder what was right and wrong, and perhaps seek out other mice who were more knowledgeable about the customs of mice. Of course, animals live in a continual childhood and have no opportunity of developing consciousness. They never experience this shift in intelligence.

In this second phase, it is the absence of certainty that gradually dawns on us, thankfully not all of a sudden, and the uncertainly urges us to seek and engage in the exploration of self. In adolescence, we are caused to ask "why" not to explain life away but to rejoin the fields of intelligence from which we have become detached. It is the genius of the evolutionary process that when certainty is removed humans are forced to engage by their own will and choice.

Unfortunately, modern education and the prevalent IQ bias encourage us to give up the power of choice and adopt a role or place in society before we have explored our great potential. We are given a false certainty that if we follow the system everything will turn out fine. As we know, the crises that so many people face in later life are the undoing of this assumed certainty.

When I do presentations about SQ around the world, I like to show two photographs of myself. In one I am aged nine, a young boy beaming with delight, open-eyed and clearly engaged. In the second I am sixteen, sitting in a café in Paris acting a part. The book I am reading (Jean-Paul Sartre, of course), the look I have adopted, the clothes I have on are all an artifice to cause effect. Most telling of all, on the inside I felt empty and lost, and that showed. If you have pictures of yourself from these ages I would strongly advise you to look at them while reading this chapter.

In the absence of a real search for self, I was learning how to use my IQ and EQ to cover up the inner sense of emptiness with a new identity. I was mastering the art of seeming to be interested in the world when I was really not engaged. The understanding of how this identity forms and excludes us from future intelligent growth will be dealt with in the next chapter.

As much as I yearned to become something great, I was being nudged toward a decision (EQ) about available options (IQ), rather than toward choosing any original formation of self (SQ).

No experience conveyed this better than a day at school when I was thirteen years old. Each member of the class was granted an interview with a careers advisory officer to determine the path in life that would be best for us to follow according to our intelligence and inclination. I was presented with an A–Z of career paths: astronomer, botanist, chemist, doctor, all the way through to zoologist. I was invited to decide which of these options most appealed to me, with some impatient persuading from the adviser.

Each career was a chance to find certainty in what someone had done before me and not to be lost. Yet an inner voice kept saying, "But why? Why become an Egyptologist or a French teacher?" I needed to find some continuity with the inner part of my life thus far, some "why" that intelligently chose to affirm what I was (the nature that had formed in my childhood years) and what I was to become, not a role that I was to inhabit either coldly or warmly.

Without finding some continuity of self from childhood through adolescence, we cut ourselves off from our deepest resource, the SQ core that we experienced as children. In SQ training we say that there is only one choice that we ever really face in this phase and that is the choice to affirm our deeper self. I truly believe that the underlying pressures to turn our children toward careers that offer no continuity with their childhood lead to a tragic waste of the most valuable resource.

Phase Three: Adulthood

For the sake of continuity, let's move on to the third phase to complete the overall picture of the truth of the situation in which we find ourselves in. Nevertheless, bear in mind that in the next chapter we will need to take a step back.

While we may be adult physically, I want to explore the many combinations of intelligence in our lives and show that in many ways we are still adolescents facing adult challenges in a world that requires adult solutions. The promise of being lost in adolescence and becoming aware of ourselves is that we will find ourselves and discover that by this process we have become more than we were when we started out.

In the story of the prodigal son, the father is most pleased with the son because he returned by his own efforts, whereas his brothers never even left home. His journey brought consciousness of the journey itself and with it real emotional value (EQ) and wisdom (new IQ). As long as we think of our life as one thing that begins and ends we will always be striving to try to control it. It will always seem as if it is running out and that we must desperately cling to it to make it valuable.

What is the point of a life that lasts for 70 or 80 years if we have done nothing, added nothing, have only bided our time and stayed close to home, clinging to what others tell us is safe and secure? Isn't that what we all fear, living but leaving no trace?

In Figure 3 we see the SQ core expanded with a self-chosen presence of self that is mindful. It understands the truth of the situation and lives it and expresses it through feelings and wisdom.

If we have successfully fulfilled our adolescent phase and developed an SQ-engaged level of self, we can now begin to see

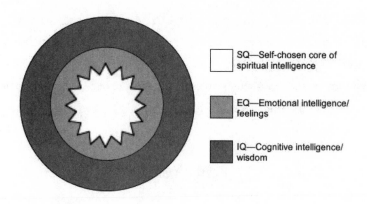

SQ—Self-chosen core of
spiritual intelligence

EQ—Emotional intelligence/
feelings

IQ—Cognitive intelligence/
wisdom

Figure 3

the way the three parts of the story unify into one great and meaningful context. This can only be seen, felt, and known by a self that has refound its own completeness (SQ, EQ, and IQ again working in harmony).

A single purpose

The overall picture of these three phases shows the coherence of life. We are born and given a start in which our core nature is the certainty that a higher field of intelligence grants us. We are then, in phase two, allowed consciously to explore and form our own unique self, a level of self that can participate both consciously and responsibly. In phase three, we can bring new intelligence into the world by our engagement in the greater fields of intelligence and offer a contribution in making things new and better. This is what marks a spiritually intelligent individual: they change the world, no matter to how small a degree.

These three phases represent a single purpose: to bring more conscious intelligence—more SQ—into the world. That is the situation we live in and the truth of it is present in every moment of living, wherever we are and whatever we are doing. Even sitting in a traffic jam can be a richly generative experience if we can wrestle ourselves free from the perceived injustice of why the car in front won't let us overtake.

Being lost

I believe that the truth of most people's situation is that they are stuck in adolescence, cut off from their core, living a life of quiet deceit, acting as if it they are happy when they are not, suggesting that they will do great things when they are not connected to a level of intelligence where greatness is possible. In short, they are lost.

The seven steps of spiritual intelligence described in this book are designed to assist people who have the strength to acknowledge that they no longer want to accept the adolescent self-deceit that nothing can be done and that, as much as they think they should be happy, they know they are not. The pursuit of happiness does not begin with the pursuit of happiness; it begins with the brave acknowledgment that we are actually lost.

Being lost is not a state of affairs with which we have been educated to feel at ease, but it is a vital awareness of self. Being aware of the challenge is 90 percent of overcoming it. The following story makes the point so well:

One day an Englishman was wandering through the countryside of the West of Ireland on his way to the town of Galway. He was lost in the hills and valleys and saw what he thought must be a local person, sat on top of a fence chewing a piece of straw. Heading toward the man, the Englishman asked: "Can you tell me where I might find the road to Galway?"

"Why yes, of course," replied the Irishman, surveying the landscape ahead. "Take this path down by the church and walk a mile or so along, until you come across a small pond." All of a sudden he stopped. "No, no, no. Now that I think of it, you'd be better off going down this other path toward the pub and along the little stream on your left for a mile or so when you'll come to an old oak tree." Again he stopped and seemed perplexed. "How difficult can it be?" the Englishman urged him on."Which of these routes will best get me there?"

"Well," the Irishman answered, "if I were you, I wouldn't be starting from here at all."

If the Englishman did find his way to Galway, would he be any the less lost? Isn't that the joke? When we think that if only this or that happened we would no longer feel inner anxiety or even depression, then we are lost.

The paradox is that we need to find SQ to be able to find SQ. It cannot be found by the "what" road, nor can it be found by the "how" road. How do I find happiness, success, peace, settlement? The answer to all is the same: If I were you I wouldn't start from here.

Empty inside

Some years ago, I was making a presentation at a conference in the Netherlands. As anyone who works with people knows, one of the privileges of doing this is that it can be a wonderful feedback system that helps us to fashion and fine tune our work and see what we cannot see when we are alone. It can also be sobering to realize that as good as we think we are, we are sometimes self-deceiving. I always make a point of dividing my time between writing and lecturing for this reason.

At the end of one particular session, a man came up to me and asked if I could spare half an hour, as he wanted to discuss certain aspects of my work. His manner caught me. He was both sincere and troubled. I walked with him to the hotel adjoining the conference center and we sat down in the coffee lounge.

This man was what might generally be regarded as a leader of people. He had been to business school, had a background in international law, worked swiftly through the ranks, took supplementary training in speech and presentation skills, body language disciplines, and interpersonal skills, courses in how to order written and spoken material, in how to conduct meetings, interviews, shareholder gatherings, and so on. He had done it all.

In addition, I had found him to be decent, principled, and he had a definite charisma that one might associate with leadership. He expected to be heard and he expected himself to have something valuable to say. He was in his late 40s. He told me that it was unusual for him not to feel in control, but in the light of my presentation he wanted to tell me a story and asked if I would listen. This is the story he related to me, with no more formal introduction than that.

"You know, a strange thing occurred," he began. "A couple of days ago, I was standing in front of a gathering of about 150 people who had come to hear about the merger of our company with another large concern. I was in full stride; the charts were projected on the wall behind. I've done this kind of thing a hundred times and I have a great deal of experience in presentations. I was engaging the audience, careful to warm them to the topic, to give them an overall picture of what I was going to cover.

"I had several succinct points to run through and I told them so. It was going well and smoothly, when I had an uncanny sensation as if I was no longer doing the presentation. It was like some part of me had left my body and was watching me as if I was one of the audience. I saw the postures, heard the tones of voice, at one moment full of charm, at the next full of persuasion, controlling but with enough studied humor not to seem dominant—letting them seem to be in control of the situation, when really I was pulling every string.

"I saw myself and I saw through myself. The presentation looked slick, but it was terribly empty and without meaning. This must have gone on for a good two or three minutes, and when I pulled myself back to reality, if that is what it is, I realized that I had been on automatic and that the speech had scarcely skipped a beat. That was the point, it was automatic. It was unreal!

"Strangely, at the end of the speech no one had noticed this strange separation but me. It has bothered me for the last couple of days. What really troubled me was that I didn't truly believe in a single thing I was saying. I had learnt the outer form or skill of the art, but I seemed to have lost myself and I saw that. I was like an empty shell, even though people came up to me after the applause to tell me how impressed they had been. I told myself I couldn't go on like this, but I knew that in milder forms I had met this point a thousand times before. Yes, I could go on, that was the frightening thing; I could go on and on and had done. But on this occasion I chose not to.

"Until today I thought that not to go on was a failure of some sort, but now I realize that I have lost touch with why I am doing what I am doing. Inside it all, it is empty, empty, empty."

I will always remember the way he spoke those last three words—"empty, empty, empty." He told me that it was the only time he had ever felt so not in control, and yet it was the first time for years that he had felt really engaged. "This realization made me feel more alive than any success I have ever had on stage," he added.

I can only praise this man's accomplishment. To have done so much and be willing to acknowledge that something else was now needed in his life was impressive and in that I saw the beginning signs of real self-leadership. He continued his work, but over the next year underwent a very deep transformation and became something of an SQ leader in my mind.

From adolescence to adulthood

The development from adolescence, phase two, to true adulthood, phase three, begins with a deep sense of being unconditionally lost and accepting it. And this acceptance does not come from the inner calculation that "I don't really quite know where I am at the moment but I am sure that if only I did A or B then I would have C some time in the future and then I would no longer feel lost (or unhappy, unfulfilled, depressed)."

Reasonable and compelling as these arguments can be, the truth of the situation is not up around the bend, it is in the here and now and it is only in the here and now that its full impact can be felt. Understanding is, as the word compound indicates, standing under. When we stand under the SQ fields of intelligence we get new perceptions that are never available "some time in the future." SQ is a live engagement.

When we stand under our previous solutions we get a new version of them. Until we are willing to give up the assumption that everything will somehow turn out fine, we will continue to be set apart from a live engagement with the greater truth of the situation.

We are locked in Figure 2. We are adolescent as individuals and as a society, applying adolescent solutions to adult problems. Unless we acknowledge that, we cannot evolve to become the full potentiality that we find in Figure 3—the adult human. The underlying journey from adolescence to adulthood is the basis of the seven steps, which form a template of rebuilding access to our full intelligence capability.

Biologically we grow old, but growing old has no meaning unless it is accompanied by inner development. Getting old requires only endurance and survival, whereas becoming adult needs inner growth and evolution.

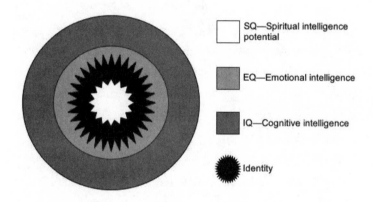

Figure 4

Figure 4 introduces the concept of the *identity*. Think of it as the ego or personality in the general sense of the term: an identification of self with body, possessions, behaviors, background, perceived accomplishments, and self-image.

Just as we have a body image that can be mentally traced even when we close our eyes, so we have a self-image that sustains itself even when evidence for it is completely lacking. Interestingly, people who have lost limbs still trace the "complete" body image, drawing in the phantom limbs where their arm or leg once was.

Nor is the identity or self-image necessarily real or accurate. It is sustained because that is what we believe ourselves to be. It is formed in phase two by the absence of any real life engagement. The identity is an "as if" life. It combines IQ and EQ, but without a real core of meaning. No doubt if I had not been faced with my own self-deceit I would today be a philosophy professor taking myself very seriously indeed.

It is our identity that causes us not to be able to stand under the unlimited intelligence fields of SQ. It blocks the flow of connection to any higher intelligence. In fact, the identity has an intelligence that continually ensures that it is not exposed to any higher or greater truth. The identity is the restless life that always thinks of one more scheme or short cut or quick fix to make things work. Being lost in the SQ sense is inwardly acknowledging that the identity cannot find any new level and that only by "deenveloping" the influence of the identity can we reengage at a new level.

The deceitful identity

The identity imprisons or envelops our SQ core in the same way that kidnappers hold a hostage to ransom. The kidnappers keep the hostage alive and use the hostage's value to the outside world as a means of bargaining for their own ends. They have no self-value except through being able to bargain for the release of the hostage. They are protected as long as they keep their prey alive and their intelligence is honed to this result, always promising to release the hostage while exacting an ever higher price for that release.

The identity intercepts every attempt from the inner or outer world to communicate with the SQ core. In this way, when the SQ seeks to get free and grow by engaging, the intelligence of the identity will try to ensure that it is thwarted with all kinds of deceit and false promises. How many times have we felt an inner urge to change and break free, only for it to be overlaid by further protestations that "now is not the time." The identity promises to get real "when things are settled at home," "when the work situation balances out a bit," "when I am financially secure." It uses anything from threat to balm to promises to keep the inner core confined.

We are the hostage keepers of our own higher intelligent self, with guilt and blame (low EQ) acting as our two emotional sentinels. Our identity repeats the same old answers to the same old problems as we continually fall short of ever growing to new or meaningful levels.

In psychology this process is termed denial. Brain scientist V. S. Ramachandran refers to this kind of denial in terms of hemi-neglect, one hemisphere in denial of what to the other hemisphere (and to others) is obviously the case. The dominant left hemisphere becomes blind to the obvious contrary evidence that the right hemisphere perceives. In just the same way, our self-image can be woefully fantastic and unreal, but it manages to navigate through life, avoiding ever being confronted.

The identity needs to use deceit as a way of sustaining and stabilizing its view of the world. It continues to sustain the outer persona that everything is fine in spite of overwhelming evidence to the contrary. It is only when the evidence of a greater truth becomes so monumental that the previous paradigm of viewing breaks down. This is the positive aspect of crisis, when crisis is accompanied by real engagement. Of course, if there is no engagement in a new paradigm then all kinds of psychological and mental instability ensue. I am very wary of techniques that purport to break down these barriers without understanding the complexity of the process.

Freud called this kind of engagement the "dethronement of man." He held that the single common denominator in all great scientific revolutions was the breakdown of some assumed and self-deceiving position of human supremacy. I prefer to call it a process of deenvelopment (or development). When we become released from the false identity that sustains deceit (what we think is the truth of our situation), by deenveloping what surrounds the bright SQ core (Figure 4), it does not merely act as a dethronement, it also acts in releasing the inner brilliance of life.

The revolutions (I prefer to call them evolutions) to which Freud points include the Copernican revolution, in which we are forced to acknowledge that the earth is not the center of the universe; the Darwinian revolution, in which our evolutionary credentials are questioned; and his own discovery of the "unconscious," in which the illusion that we are in charge of our lives is undermined.

To this list I would add the current existential crisis that we face and our potential release into a new age of intelligent spirituality and meaning. We must expect to face ourselves, our self-assumed identities, and to deenvelop from their influence if we are to release this great inner potentiality. We must face what we have become and release what we can yet become. We cannot "get" spiritual intelligence like we can get a driver's license or a PhD, we have to release it, awaken it, engage with it—even remember it.

Deenveloping the identity

The seven steps of spiritual intelligence show the way to deenvelop the grip that identity has on our core and reengage us in the pursuit of a mindful self that is the promise of adolescence, as we saw in Figure 2.

You don't need to give up work and retreat to the mountains to take your self apart. Continue on the outside as normal, but begin to observe and understand the situation. Reforming your self is an inside job.

Become aware of the deceit. Make it an exercise in observing. The seven steps are full of simple ways. The identity wants us to sleep, not to question, not to strive, not to affirm the greatness that we are. It is a lie that we must learn to detect and in so doing be able to listen to the quiet beyond the restless noise. We need to remember our self. Every platitude spoken, old solution offered, or careless reaction provoked is a victory for the identity.

As many great spiritual traditions have shown, the difficulty is that we are so attached to the deceit that we protect it: we think it *is* our self. To detect our lies is to expose who we have come to believe we are and there will be a feeling of tearing from the attachment as this happens. We are not searching for the problem, we embody the problem.

Somewhere in our self we know that we have had a hand in covering up the rarest and most precious jewel of all—the opportunity of our self. Have we not developed an entire language and behavior to cover up the first lie? Settling for our lot, getting by, making the best of things all cover up the intense and compelling opportunity of life that we feel inside. We have all sold out at one point or another and reasoned that because we can't find the great mission of life that we felt was our future in phase two, we should at least try to make the best of things as they are.

We have buried the truth somewhere inside. It needs to be shallow enough to be able to be retrieved and yet deep enough not to be able to be detected by others. This is why I use the word deceit. Somewhere inside, we know that our life can be so much more and that we have sold ourselves the lie (or been sold it) that we have to settle for less.

If figures on stress, depression, anxiety, and the experience of an "existential vacuum" are to be believed, it seems that a very different condition underlies the outer persona on which we have built an entire culture. Even the most successful and rich are struggling to be happy. The collective lie is becoming so overwhelming that we can no longer sustain it.

The seven steps of spiritual intelligence seek both to reestablish the intelligence of higher meaning at the core of our self, and simultaneously to deenvelop the impediments of our identity.

As we begin to acknowledge that what we have thought of as our self may in large part be a fabrication and a cover-up, a get-by identity, we will begin to experience the freedom that belongs with adolescence evolving to new realms of opportunity in our adulthood. The opportunity lies exactly where we don't think to look—in among our problems, inside the life that we already lead.

This is the story of the seven steps ahead. You may find it useful to return to the diagrams of the phases of life each time you pick up and continue reading. Each time we construct the three-phased "truth of the situation" in our mind, we invite a united thinking process, an exploratory frame of mind. The more we exercise this faculty of intelligence, the more it strengthens the presence of our mind, and the more we will be able to see the truth of our situation inside our everyday life.

Part II

Taking the Seven Steps

The seven steps of spiritual intelligence

Step One: Awareness—We become aware that we are lost, that we do not understand the purpose of our life, that this internal, "not knowing" sense is in fact the real sense of self confined by the lack of any intelligence to escape.

Step Two: Meaning—We explore the bigger picture, to make keys that might open the space we are confined in.

Step Three: Evaluation—We try the keys, fit them in the lock and turn.

Step Four: Being Centered—We open the door inward and enable what is on the other side to access us.

Step Five: Vision—We allow the light from the new, "bigger picture" to flood in so we can see.

Step Six: Projection—We project our new level of self into the new territory we can see ahead.

Step Seven: Mission—We act within the new territory and are now aware and conscious of what we are doing within a greater territory.

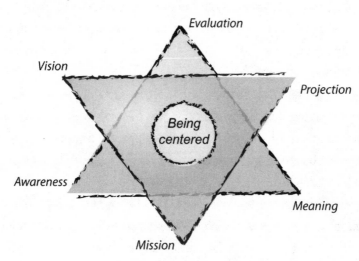

Each chapter in the journey of the seven steps will begin with a "signpost" stating where the chapter is heading. These signposts only name the territory that lies ahead—they are not the journey itself. They state the obvious, but that sometimes only seems obvious once you have seen it, so you may find it useful to read the signposts not only before the chapter but also again afterward.

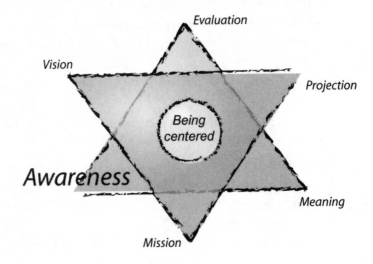

In this first step, we are going to look at how the truth of our situation is ever present and would catch our attention were we not so preoccupied, so aware of the wrong things in the wrong way, so distracted and absent.

By training ourselves to become aware of the wholeness of life within the truth of the situation, we develop the presence of this as a context for our mind. This develops a very different kind of awareness in the way we watch, listen, or sense life around us and within ourselves.

Whether it is being aware of another person, an issue, a challenge we face, or the growth of our inner self, in the presence of SQ we come to realize that all life is seeking to grow, to join and become part of something more than itself.

5

Step One: Awareness

The notes I handle no better than many pianists. But the pauses between the notes—ah, that is where the art resides.

Pianist Artur Snabel

In 1893 the young Mohandas Gandhi has just arrived in South Africa and is traveling on a train to his first official meeting as an attorney. He has come from India to provide his legal services to Indians abroad. He is sitting in a first-class compartment, at one moment reading and at another taking in the scenery of this new land. He is blissfully unaware of the racial attitudes in the country and that it is forbidden for a "colored" to be traveling first class.

A white ticket collector enters the compartment with an indignant white passenger in tow, demanding to know what a "coolie" is doing there and how he got a first-class ticket. At first Gandhi fails to understand the question. "I am an attorney and I got the ticket through the post" is his innocent explanation.

An absurd conversation ensues. The white passenger maintains, to Gandhi's face, that there are no colored attorneys in South Africa. The terms attorney and colored are mutually exclusive in a white-controlled apartheid country. Gandhi persists that he is an attorney, enrolled at the High Court of Chancellery in London, and if he is perceived to be colored then, his argument proceeds, there clearly is at least one colored attorney in South Africa.

This is too much for the irate passenger and he brusquely instructs the ticket collector to throw Gandhi off the train. Before Gandhi can complete his objections, he finds himself unceremoniously pushed out of the door at the next station. In the film *Gandhi*, the camera pans back at this moment to show a sweep of the station where Gandhi is lying sprawled on the darkened platform, his suitcase thrown on top of him, and out of the window of the departing train the gloating, leering faces of the ticket collector and the other white passengers, pleased to be rid of this "coolie."

Gandhi seethes with resentment. With the fire of indignation burning in his eyes, the young attorney picks himself up, trying to regain some composure; he brushes his suit down and looks around to see where he is. The sign says "Maritzburg," an unknown place in an unfamiliar country. This is as much as he can perceive of his situation at that moment. Then, out of the corner of his eye, his attention is caught by a poor black family, mother, father, and baby huddled at the back of the platform after leaving the third-class section of the train. They are dark shapes being swallowed by the dark night. Here, one senses, Gandhi sees the real poverty and squalor, the real oppressed people of South Africa.

He turns, first toward the departing train where he feels the personal insult at his treatment, and then back to the man, woman, and baby who do not have the luxury of resentment, they have food and shelter to find. At this moment, Gandhi sinks to his knees. Even in his posture, he has acquiesced to a greater truth than that which avenging personal insult or feeling sympathy for those less fortunate would express. He is being made aware of something far greater in this situation.

This awareness is not alarmist, is not calling out for a quick solution. It awakens in Gandhi issues that pertain to the real "laws" of life rather than the legal niceties of what has just occurred to him. His life is being awakened not just in regard to this particular situation and the details of his plight or even the plight of this one poor family, but to a much, much bigger issue: why we are here and what we are here to do. He was, in a very real and metaphorical sense, changing trains.

Many years later, Louis Fischer recounted, in his biography of Gandhi, how Dr. John Mott, a Christian missionary, asked Gandhi what had been the most creative experience of his life. In reply Gandhi told the story of that night at Maritzburg station. Apparently he had stayed there the whole night through, crouched on the platform and shivering in the freezing cold, unable through shyness or shock even to reach for his overcoat.

I would count this scene as one of the most eloquent expressions of what I call the spiritually intelligent level of awareness. It is the starting point of the journey of our self as it grows with spiritual intelligence.

What is awareness?

We are aware all the time but, as we shall see, we are mostly aware of the wrong things in the wrong way, too alert and too much prone to a sense of emergency or a need to act and react. We are often unaware that a greater truth may be pressing to catch our attention. Real awareness is always awakening to that which we haven't yet seen or heard or noticed. It is always a new journey beginning.

We understand awareness in general terms as the process whereby our nervous system acts as a kind of motorway for incoming impressions to the brain, which are translated into auditory, visual, olfactory, or kinesthetic information; the senses are what we normally think of as the main pathways by which we are made aware of the world around us. Awareness promotes recognition, associations, memories, it can trigger reactions, stimulate dialog, the remembrance of behavior, faces, memories…

If we take a moment and quite literally listen to the noise inside our heads, the inner dialog that is stimulated from both within and without, we may get some idea of the sheer amount of traffic the brain is processing.

But this cannot be the whole picture. In addition to being made aware of the world, inside and outside, there is the self, the observer, the potential actor in the affairs of living. Antonio Damasio, one of the world's leading experts on the neuro-physiology of emotions, expresses it thus: "The presence of you in a particular relationship with some object. If there was no such presence, how would your thoughts belong to you?"

Fight, flight, and awareness

As we shall see in this and the subsequent steps, the level of self that acts can either be our self-identity or our developing con-sciousness of a new level of self. Our self-identity (remember Fig-ure 4) is an actor that has been trained to survive in the absence of the growth of the SQ core. It is our self as long as we don't choose our greater self. It uses our systems, our emotional intel-ligence, and our IQ, but it has no progression itself. It handles the world, it can be cunning, it can act in a considerate way, it can be smart or not, but it is essentially fixed, habitual, and repetitive.

The SQ self is always seeking growth and development. It is a growing presence that develops a meaningful relationship with the world and all it encounters. It grows by being engaged in the truth of the situation and not by merely surviving.

In the example of the young Gandhi at the railway station, we see both of these actors. There is first the self-identity that reacts in fight and flight to the guard and passengers on board the train and then to the black family disappearing into the shadows. He wants to fight and then he transforms his anger into a concern for others, an emotional strategy that can be a valid flight reaction. Then we see another feature of the autonomic nervous system (I will go into this in more detail later), where Gandhi engages in a greater truth than the fight or flight response. He is awakened to the core of self as being a space that is searching, questioning, wondering why. It doesn't know how to act, doesn't even know itself, but it is, without doubt, highly engaged.

We know that our nervous system, when it reads the cues of present danger, reacts with flight and fight. We also know that the danger need not be real. It is enough that we perceive it to be real. The more entrenched our self-identity, the more we are likely to read anything that is different or unusual as a threat to that entrenched level of identity. The more quickly we react with fight and flight to what we don't understand, what is new, what doesn't conform to our opinions, the less developed is our inner sense of our SQ core. It is the SQ intelligence that is at ease with the new, unusual, what is yet to be known. The identity tries to keep everything the same.

The identity uses our EQ and IQ intelligence to ensure that the greater truth of the situation is not allowed to touch us—

it wants to preserve itself at all costs. When we are aware of the inner space that is the natural domain of the SQ self, we also become aware of how our identity uses the intelligences in our system to cover up the greater truth of the situation. Doing nothing at such moments can be the most effective strategy of all. Given time, new awareness will dawn.

Between fight and flight, there is what is characterized as a "relaxed state" in the autonomic nervous system. When the storms of life abate and we feel safe, we tend to act like any animal in retreat, taking food and comforting diversions into our "cave." For the human animal this may be closing the door on the world, lying on a sofa flicking through television channels with some snacks at hand, safe at last from the rough and tumble of the day.

As humans, we are uniquely placed not just to be aware, but to be aware of our awareness. This faculty enables us to intervene between incoming impressions and our reactions. We can pause for thought, register sounds, sights, and smells, process them and mentally take ourselves away from the immediate reactions of our identity and observe the scene of which we are a part. With practice we can extend the period between action and reaction.

For instance, imagine you are on a long and boring bus journey with no book to read, no points of interest, and no immediate prospect of arriving at your destination. As the bus wends its way along, you gaze detachedly out of the window and see the fields, the passing skyline, the clouds forming, people going about their business, all at a relaxed, unthreatening pace.

Then at some point you become alerted to a detail, prompted from inside or outside yourself. Perhaps you notice a mother tending her baby and this triggers recollections of your own childhood. Then this moment of awareness passes and you return to gazing at the scenery, only for this state again to be supplanted by another detail in your surroundings that alerts you. We can move to and from the relaxed and alert states for ever, but this is not being aware.

Real awareness is a deliberate engagement. It breaks the patterns of life that gravitate around the identity of self feeling comfortable and relaxed. It challenges the assumption that all is fine, that life will turn out well in the end. Real awareness exposes the superficiality of face-value actions with which the identity is preoccupied, such as seeming to be interested in the mother and baby or the scenery.

The SQ individual is willing to resist the "relaxed" state that is a soporific balm and to choose to use whatever means will awaken the self to the great challenges and adventures of an unfolding and evolving life.

The space within

Many years ago, during a summer recess from university in Montreal, I took a bus ride around America. One memorable visit was to the Grand Canyon in Arizona. I had seen pictures of it and wanted to stand there myself.

The bus stopped about 100 meters from a stunning perspective on the canyon. The sun was setting and the passengers wandered over to catch the view.

For me it was an exhilarating experience to walk to the side of the canyon, knowing I was going to see something awesome. I was not disappointed. I could have stayed there for days. The usual noise in my head quietened and I became aware of the sheer enormity of the world and my own mortality. The sun setting and the canyon have existed for millions of years. My awareness of this was accompanied by a sense that life is finite. It quickened in me the desire to make a mark while I was alive, to live deliberately and meaningfully.

After 10 or 15 minutes, many of the party had seen the extraordinary sight and were ready to move on. "Beautiful," one man exclaimed. "So, where to next?" asked another.

Awareness can be shallow and focused only on EQ and IQ details (how big, how high, how far, how beautiful) or it can be deeply transforming. Life provides many moments every day when the greater truth of our situation impresses itself on us. It is not necessary to go to the Taj Mahal or the Grand Canyon for this to happen. What is necessary is that we do not cut ourselves off from the potential depth of our awareness.

Understanding the truth of the situation begins in being aware of a bigger picture, a state of affairs that is always the same and never changing, a permanent truth, not a passing interest. Being aware of details that pass like the ebb and flow of life is fundamentally different to being aware of self as a presence that is seeking to grow intelligence within the greatness of a world that, contrary to the way our identity behaves, is largely unknown and unexplored.

The passion we may feel in the love of an idea, an ideal, a mission can "clear the space"—or more accurately clear the identity from swamping the space—and make it possible to feel that inner presence of self that wants to grow. In a similar way, coming up against a greater experience that we cannot simply use old habits to process, such as the loss of a loved one and the grief that accompanies it, can clear away the grip our identity has on each successive moment. In the absence of being aware of ancillary details, a state is created in which our SQ intelligence can be felt and known. Love and loss are two of the great disinfectants of that inner space. A person who loves what they are doing is characterized by always being aware of new aspects, new opportunities. To work or live "because we have to" is a slow death of our inner potential.

Think of Socrates, wearing sandals, standing on a battle-field covered with snow, for a whole long day and night contemplating a particular question; or Newton, sat with rapt attention, looking at the light passing through a prism. Recall your own moments when you have been fired up by something you love to do. It is in these moments of awareness when we are struck dumb that the third, higher part of our nervous system becomes engaged. The presence of our self becomes part of the event of living.

These moments are actually more common than we think, but we are so unused to simply "being" in that state of awareness that we pass them over—looking to react, to sort out a wrong, to make a decision, to resolve the issue. Often by doing many things we only make waves; by doing a few in the same direction we can change the current of the water.

Our inner space is crowded with thousands of impressions of the world around us. We are often drowning in the intensity of impressions, yet we still try to fill in more. Even at the end of a busy day, we cannot stop reading the signs on trains and passing buses, we read articles in newspapers that have been left on vacant seats, we think about things we will never do—to ensure that the rush of impressions through our systems is sustained.

In our effort to fill our lives we have made them empty. We feel as if something is missing if the noise and pace abate even for a few moments.

The "El Bowery syndrome" is named after an area of New York. Apparently one night the usual noise of passing trains stopped due to a fault in the electrical system. Hundreds of local residents phoned the police to report an eerie something in the air. That was simply the absence of noise. We are accustomed to a certain amount of noise, just as we become accustomed to a certain weight of food in our belly and anything less leaves us feeling hungry and empty, even when we are not.

We have the choice of what we engage in and why. We are like a vacant house: if we do not choose the tenant that occupies our inner space, before long someone, anyone, will move in, take over, and claim the house as their own.

This inner space is where we can consciously choose, as if it were a garden, what to grow and what to weed out. We can be self-leaders who guide our lives in a conscious direction, rather than reactors to the endless details of life that keep us busy going nowhere.

Not being distracted

I was once presented with a very simple exercise in relation to inner space. I was instructed to walk through a shopping mall and choose not to be distracted by anything other than one thought of my choice. This is a little like the Buddhist practice of pinpoint meditation, where you empty yourself out by focusing on one thing.

I chose to focus on an issue that was of particular interest to me at the time and set off through a local shopping mall. I had not gone one meter when a brightly colored orange and red sign offering a 50 percent reduction on the price of suits and shirts caught my attention. True to the rules of the exercise, I walked back and started again.

On the next attempt I was distracted by the inner aware-ness of my inner dialog that had tried *not* to be distracted by a sign offering 50 percent off suits and shirts! In all the attempts I made in over an hour, I never got more than about 15 meters along the mall. In turn distracted, dispersed, disturbed, alerted, accelerated, irritated, aggravated, aggrieved, and much more, my identity set my emotions running ever hotter at each successive attempt.

Some weeks later I visited friends who had just had a baby daughter. She was only a few days old and I was quite taken aback at how much of an impression she made on me. I found myself thinking about what she would face growing up in today's world.

After an hour or so I left their house and felt like walking. I had left my car at home and, rather than take the train, I walked on past the station, and on and on. Suddenly, I found myself walking out beyond the city limits and I realized that no shop, no person, no advertising slogan had penetrated my awareness. I had even passed the same shopping area where I had tried not to be interested in the brightly colored sale signs.

When I had dwelt in a permanent truth, I was able to sustain an inner focus of awareness for hours, but when I had tried not to be aware of the world around I had become doubly aware of everything that distracted me. Trying not to think about problems or bad situations doesn't make them go away, nor does thinking about them and trying to solve them. We have to allow the greater truth of the situation to impress us and engage us. That is the best protection from distractions.

Brain science shows us what and how—but not why

There is a simple notion in brain science that has made its way into our common vocabulary, "working memory." New York University neuroscientist Joseph le Doux describes how working memory operates:

Working memory is pretty much what used to be called short-term memory. However, the term working memory implies not just a temporary storage system but an active processing mechanism used in thinking and reasoning ... Working memory, in short, sits at the crossroads of bottom-up and top-down processing systems and makes high-level thinking and reasoning possible.

If we were to build a cupboard, we would need to keep inside our working memory the details of the tools that would be required, the materials, the glue, the nails, the wood, the overall construction. We could build up the cupboard from the materials, the tools, the design, and so on, or we could have the finished cupboard in our mind, see what is needed, and work down. The working memory, as Le Doux describes it, works both top down and bottom up.

Figure 5 is a simple description of how working memory operates, showing the space that is in turn influenced by the immediate context of the previous moment and the potential of what the previous moment may invite to join it. As an example, let's say there is a blue object in front of me, from which a small stream of smoke is emerging. I recognize it as a cup of tea. Once I do so, the working memory is likely to be more aware of those things that a cup of tea may call for or associate with—say, a plate of biscuits or a bowl of sugar or some sandwiches.

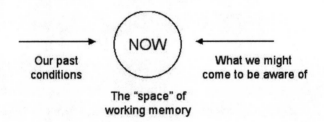

Figure 5 Working memory

This same principle applies in existential issues. Let's say you are having an argument with someone. You are more likely to be aware of the things that argument invites in your associative mind: not being understood, disagreement, anger, and so on.

This is an important piece in understanding the truth of our situation. If each previous moment conditions how we are made aware of the next moment, then we need a new starting point to escape this vicious circle. If our yesterdays condition our sense of "now" and our sense of "now" either cuts us off from or makes us prone to the content of our "tomorrows" as perceived by our "yesterdays," how is change possible? How is new opportunity ever to inform us?

Dr. Christine Northrup takes this insight one step further in saying:

> *Our central nervous system and sense organs function in such a way as to choose and process only those stimuli that reinforce what we already believe.*

Choose to engage

Give yourself some quiet time—say, five minutes two or three times a day (first thing in the morning is a good time)—and try to listen in a broad way to your inner space by asking yourself "What is the truth of the situation now?" Picture Figures 1, 2, and 3 and sense and know how much more there is to know and to do.

Don't expect an answer immediately, but listen in a broad way for something to appear in your awareness, as you might wait for the sun to rise by looking broadly at the horizon. It isn't in an exact time or place where the sun rises that the event is, but rather it's an overall event where a glow of light seems to suffuse broadly across the whole landscape.

Thinking that we already know is the most closing mental attitude to knowing anything more. The one thing we do know is that starting in our usual place is not the right place to begin. To choose to know that we don't know is a brave strategy. Remember Socrates' wonderful maxim: "I know nothing except the fact of my ignorance."

The beginning of an SQ level of self is to be discovered inside each and every moment—if we can find it. It does not require that we try harder or get away for a break. It needs us to become aware that a different intelligence system is ever present—if we can be aware, listen, and acknowledge it. It is an intelligence system that is not based in the past nor in the future but in the moment.

Try to listen beyond the noise. Be aware that this inner and outer traffic passes by, but by virtue of that inner space we have the choice whether to be involved in it or not. We cannot change the traffic, but we can develop the level of self that listens beyond the distracting noise.

Exercises

Each chapter in the seven steps is accompanied by practical exercises. These are of two kinds:

❖ Deenvelopment: those designed to deenvelop the grip of our assumed identity.

❖ Development: those designed to develop the influence of SQ intelligence at core.

Each deenvelopment exercise on the left-hand page has a corresponding development exercise on the right-hand page. Just ceasing to let the identity influence you, your potential, and your capability is not enough. You also have to find and engage new potentials in the field of intelligence.

These exercises are all based in the same principles: the conscious release from identity and the conscious choice of engagement.

DEENVELOPMENT EXERCISES

1   Detach yourself consciously from the flood of trivial impressions that fill your mind. This is done by just noting the noise that passes through the brain. Be aware of it and try not to react by fighting to stop the noise or by trying *not* to have the noise. When you stop trying you will become aware of a quiet space beyond. The challenge is not to stop the noise—it is to stop yourself engaging in it.

2   Practice distancing yourself from the traffic of internal impressions and watch them as if you were an observer. In time they become less influential on the state of your mind and you can separate the traffic from the mind itself. This carries with it the sense of watching or observing yourself and noting when you get personally involved. Unless it is something you have to deal with, leave it alone.

3   Become aware of those triggers that involve you in unnecessary things, with people and situations that you know will lead nowhere. Become aware of how you have developed pressured, demanding, and punishing attitudes that are always full of noise and traffic. Notice how the tensions and conflicts that you suffer manifest in different areas of your body. The build up of toxicity in the muscles is a static energy that reflects a lack of engagement. The more you are engaged in the bigger picture, the more your body is eased and feels well. The more you are stuck and repeating the same identity patterns, the more static gets locked into your body.

DEVELOPMENT EXERCISES

1   Practice being aware of the space within which the self is present in every moment. This is done by beginning to become aware that you don't have to act, react, reply to someone's acts or words or the flood of impressions. Just practice this until you become aware that there is an internal space. Don't engage in unnecessary things like other people's arguments or yesterday's (or today's) newspaper unless you choose to.

2   Become aware of the issues that actually catch your mind and engage you, not those that are forced on your mind. If you are caught by faces, behaviors, or leadership styles, reframe the awareness into a searching question: "I wonder why people pay attention to this person whenever they speak?" "I wonder why things always end up in conflict when …?" Ask yourself the question again and again until your mind begins to catch the freedom to search. It is probably locked and suffocating from lack of space.

3   Develop a "state of awareness" that remembers to remember the link that exists between your mind and your body. How you feel and the energy levels you have is a direct result of the way you engage in the bigger picture (or not!). Your behavior, the way you use your voice, your posture—all this can become a chosen response in time, once you have become aware of the field of intelligence in which body and mind are not separate.

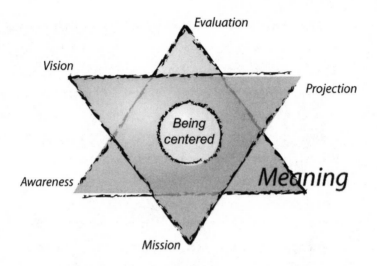

The shift from an SQ kind of awareness (Step One) reveals a whole new realm of meaning that we can so easily miss when we are caught up in the stress and overreactivity that we suffer every day when we are disengaged from our core.

In a disengaged state we tend to think of things having meaning by attaching an emotional or mental value to them. When we say that this or that *means* a lot to us because we love it (EQ) or because we think it is important (IQ), this confuses emotional and mental attachment with real meaning.

The inner sense of SQ meaning is deeply satisfying and enriching. It carries with it a sense of belonging and being part of something greater than our local situation. In our awareness of the truth of the situation, even our struggles and difficulties have meaning.

6

Step Two: Meaning

We feel that even when all possible scientific questions have been
answered, the problems of life remain completely untouched.
Ludwig Wittgenstein

In 1917 T. E. Lawrence—Lawrence of Arabia, as he comes to be known—is working in a shabby office playing no obvious part in the First World War, yet his attention is on the unfolding events, specifically operations in the Arab countries. He is not distracted but alert, awake and poised—and the meaning of his life is beginning to take shape.

Little by little, Lawrence's part becomes clear. The British are conducting a war on several fronts. The Turks are a problem, and the Arab people who could help by attacking the Turks are largely divided and without leadership. The British government is pondering how to use the Arab tribes to help them put the Turks out of the war. Lawrence will enter that debate and fill that space with a very particular significance and in a way that barely a single army general could conceive.

At a particular point in the film *Lawrence of Arabia*, Lawrence is working with an assistant, Michael George Hartley, when another assistant, William Potter, enters the room bearing the day's newspapers and fresh news of the war.

Lawrence takes the newspaper and is absorbed in reading it. "Tribes attack Turkish stronghold. And I bet that no one in the whole of this headquarters knows about it," he says, barely audibly.

William Potter stands idly by and is about to light a cigarette with a match. Lawrence interrupts. "Allow me," he says, lights the cigarette with the match and then holds the latter up in the air, gazing at it and beyond as one might across a desert landscape. With the thumb and index finger of his other hand, he slowly and deliberately extinguishes the flame. Both Potter and Hartley look on astonished. A few moments pass and Potter cannot resist. He takes a match and lights it and with a gaze less of the visionary and more of the mischievous schoolboy, tries to do the same. This time the reaction is predictable: "Ouch!"

"What's the trick then?" asks Potter, expecting an answer as tangible as the burning sensation in his fingers.

"The trick, William Potter," replies Lawrence, "is not minding that it hurts."

Lawrence, like many great individuals who understand the power of imagery, was a consummate showman. But the meaning of his small theatrical demonstration is clear. Training ourselves not to let our mind be formed by the small things—in his case the pain of being burnt—allows more space to be occupied with things that have real import.

This scene is a portent of things to come. It describes the difference between the individual who translates everything into their small world (identity) and the individual who translates their small world into the bigger picture. What appears as a small, almost insignificant exchange has a meaning that distinguishes between a life that merely repeats itself and a life that continually grows in significance. Who remembers William (not Harry) Potter?

It is only by the elevation of self to a new level in the great chain of being that great things can be accomplished. "Not minding" is the SQ art of being released from the material reaction, just as minding too much about the material level makes for a meaningless self that is imprisoned at that level.

It is through no obvious outward ambition that Lawrence makes his way to center stage, in fact he almost seems to stumble from one experience to another, but by his inner sensitivity and ability to be awakened and catch the meaning of events as they occur, events that bureaucracy and governmental structure simply cannot grasp in their overly reactive conduct, he stays in tune with the unfolding story in an ever-expanding picture.

Always the free-thinking individual, Lawrence is outside the system and engages in world events from a sense of being awakened to their meanings, while never having to react from and solve the daily problems by which bureaucracy is swamped in the complexities of war. Such was the dynamic of the conflict that it took a Lawrence to understand the war in other than the terms of reaction and counter-reaction. He perceived other meanings, other opportunities to act.

The film tells the story of how Lawrence leads the Arab revolt against the Turks, a turning point in the war, and makes a famous charge on the sea port of Akaba. An English officer in Arab dress on a donkey crossing the Sinai desert leading the many desert tribes in one unified action to take the Turkish city— hardly a battle plan hatched at HQ.

Lawrence leads the charge from the desert side, long believed to be inaccessible. He challenges the general assumption.

"Why can the desert not be crossed?" Lawrence persistently asks.

"Because it is written," replies Ali, the Arab leader.

"Nothing is written," says Lawrence.

That is the way of meaning—it must be found fresh each time. What we assume can and can't be done sets the confines of what will be done.

Positive meaning is always a growth of the awareness into a bigger picture, whereas reactive meaning is always a cut-off from the bigger picture, an attempt to survive, to preserve the inner identity of self. The more personally attached we are to our experiences, the more we are prone to detach ourselves from their greater meaning and repeat what we are comfortable with.

Many men and women who have all the outward trappings of success can be as trapped as if they were in a prison cell and yet no one knows it. Many times I have heard people make comments like: "You have everything, great family, great job, great house, great kids, people respect you. How can you feel empty inside? It doesn't make any sense." We are trapped because we feel that our life is written, that it cannot escape the conformity or predictability of the script it is following. Some people argue again and again with partners they so want to be at peace with, just as others repeat patterns of short-term success followed by searing disasters in business or relationships.

We confuse meaning with those things that we think are either meaning giving or that we derive meaning from: great house, great job, even great kids. Meaning is a function of the growth of the inner intelligence into a bigger picture. Meaning cannot be added in to an action that is empty. The light of greatness is not reflected, it is brightness illuminated from within.

IQ/EQ will never an SQ make

I was once asked by a lecturer at a local university if I could explain to him why seemingly insignificant things can tip the balance in a person from being reasonable to being out of control.

"Can you give me an example?" I asked him.

"Take this morning. I was driving to work and I was late. Another car cut me up and I was absolutely livid. You wouldn't have recognized me—I was shouting, almost screaming at the driver. I then sat fuming behind him and I calculated that I would arrive perhaps four or five seconds later to work. Is that the reaction of a reasonable person?"

Together we looked at the inner script underlying the events he described. The more we talked about it through the IQ, EQ, and SQ intelligences, the more it made sense. The IQ/EQ self (locked out from the core by the identity), in the absence of any deeper meaning, says that it is important that we get to work, that all kinds of things depend on us doing so that make it important not just for us but for others who rely on us because what we are doing is so important. If another driver challenges that inner dialog by cutting us up, they become responsible for diminishing the importance, the assumed value of the identity, that the chain of events supports.

The SQ individual looks at the way the identity constructs the inner IQ/EQ movie with itself as the hero and derives humor from seeing that this is the inner play of self, a childish intelligence that seeks recognition and respect at all costs. Mastering this identity, by being aware of it and seeing how it derives meaning, enables the SQ individual not to react to others from the written storyline of their identity. They inwardly forgive the adolescent identity of self that wants to play this part.

In a similar situation on the way to work, rather than react to every person who prevents them moving one meter forward, the SQ individual will think: "This is our time until we arrive and what happens in this space and in this time is up to us." The

SQ person will choose to use the space and time to work things out, explore, observe, be aware, evaluate, train, and develop meaning.

Whether we are in a traffic jam or on top of Mt. Everest, the truth of our situation is the same. The identity might try to "make the most of the situation" when it realizes that it is going to be stuck in traffic for the next hour, but this is very different from the SQ person who has chosen to be in the meaning of their life, in this time and in every time. "Making the most of" is an attitude of self that, like a virus, extends in time to everyone and everything. It is always a second-best time.

The bigger picture of life always probes and presses us to find new meaning. Our IQ and EQ intelligences are not designed to handle the volatile, live, ever-changing and engaging processes of the bigger picture that is the domain of our SQ.

The reactive self—an answer for everything

As a rule, the more reactive our inner identity, the less meaningful life becomes. We rush into adulthood seeking an identity and are pushed to decide as quickly as possible who we want to be, only to discover some time later that the identity we have developed is less a freedom and more a self-limiting prison.

SQ is the search for meaning and meaning is how we engage with the higher principles of the bigger picture of life. In the book I refer to "natural laws" and "higher principles" that express the greater truth of any situation, whether it be the greater truth about our age, about the conversation we are having at any given moment, about the argument that is going on, and so on. It is the sense of growing into that greater truth that we call meaning. Meaning has an inner physiology that accompanies it, a feeling of belonging, being joined, becoming or being made whole. It is uplifting and reduces depression and stress.

Finding a reason and saying I am doing this for "the bigger picture" or "because I want to create opportunity for the next generation" or "because I want to make a difference in this world" may sound good, but matters as little as what flavor of yoghurt we buy unless the origin of the statement is from the core of our self, not from the reactive self that wants to justify itself.

Adverts that highlight the plight of children in Africa may cause us to react and for a while we may want to do something about it. SQ will resist the easy reaction, recognizing that the reaction is at the same level as the problem, and will seek to understand and feel what the causes are of this plight and only then to search for the meaning. What does it mean that children are suffering in this world? What does it say to me and to my life as I try to understand this issue?

As we shall see from the unfolding of the seven steps, it is not to the immediate awareness of the children that the SQ individual reacts, but to the deeper and often far-back causes of the situation. Why has this situation come about? Why haven't I had this issue in my mind, since it is in the world of which I am part?

To have only an emotional reaction to an issue is often not just to miss its meaning but actively to seek to cut off from the discomfort that awareness of it produces in our identity. More to the point, the awareness of the plight of children in Africa did not naturally arise as an issue in our self—it took an advert to stimulate it. How can we *not* be aware of suffering children? Only by allowing the breakdown of this reactive self-identity can we find a new place to think about children from.

The fact is that we always are in the greater truth, there is meaning all around us, but are not aware (conscious) of it.

Meaning is developing consciousness of the world and all that lives within it. To think about children from the core of our self is to begin a lifetime's exploration of the why, the how, and the what of our values, considerations, and responsibilities toward children.

The importance of self or self-importance

We try to fit the bigger picture of life into our world, rather than to make sense of our world inside the bigger picture. Consider the difference between reaction and meaningful response (Figures 6 and 7).

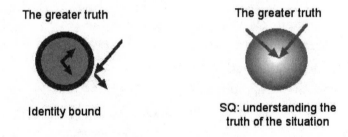

The greater truth	The greater truth
Identity bound	SQ: understanding the truth of the situation

Figure 6 The reactive self   *Figure 7 The meaningful SQ self in growth*

In Figure 6 the reactive self-identity (the thick outer circle) repels challenge from any greater truth and develops behaviors and acts both spoken and unspoken that balk at and resist anything new. It is a set and fixed mind and will not see what it doesn't want to see. It will argue needlessly, use devices to win or to ensure that it doesn't lose, it will self-deceive and cover up to survive, and put a spin on its actions that suggests it is deep, meaningful, caring, and all kinds of other qualities.

It is full of insecurity and acts in consideration of others or the world only after it feels secure in its own self-importance. It is the Hollywood movie star who, having made $20 million, decides they want to "give back to this great country." It can sound like character, but it is character in style only.

The more one acts from this identity, the more it locks the innermost potential of self; just as the more we see the hypocrisy of our actions, the more the enclosure of the inner core of self is released.

In Figure 7, the greater truth of the situation awakens the SQ core response to grow to incorporate new and unexplored levels of self. It is the growth of self into the bigger picture that provides meaning and all the attendant feelings of growth.

The SQ self seeks challenge, embraces difficulty, accepts what is, and invites feedback, reflections, uncertainty, the unknown. A spiritually intelligent self knows that it cannot be defeated, beaten, overcome, it can only grow or become locked by the absence of nutrient and light from the greater truth.

Challenge and difficulty help the SQ person keep their reactive self-identity from growing and covering up the truth of the situation. The humility of the SQ person is not an act, it is a necessary and chosen process that ensures their reactive self is ever shrunken to make more space to grow from the core to the outside.

Humor as an antidote to stubborn identity

I believe, along with leading brain researcher V. S. Ramachandran, that humor and laughter evolved as an effective way of signaling that a potential threat had passed and the way ahead was now all clear. The contagious nature of laughter can spread this "all clear" signal to the group more effectively and swiftly than any explanation. Jokes or humorous situations are often structured in such a way that a chain of events suggests an unfortunate outcome, only to be reversed by a punch line that reframes the whole meaning of what went before.

Self-deprecating humor acts in much the same way on our identity. Our identity often feels threatened and this causes it to be antagonized, to generate tension, to be ready to fight or flee, and the like. A well-timed joke about ourselves aimed at deflating an inflated ego can have the effect of relieving the grip of identity on our core. It is a highly valuable tool of self-leadership. I have often seen potentially difficult or confrontational situations defused by a good self-leader using humor in just this way.

It is a mark of great cultures and great individuals that they can laugh at themselves, just as it is a mark of adolescent cultures and individuals that they make jokes at the expense of others. In the hands of the less developed, humor becomes a weapon of the identity designed to belittle, shame, and intimidate others under the guise of "just having a joke." Good humor, on the other hand, is always unifying, allows us all to see some aspect of concealed truth, and creates an ease in which arguments, discussions, and issues are easier to handle.

The adulthood of emotions displayed by SQ individuals

There are what we might call adolescent or destructive emotions and what we may call more mature or constructive emotions. We don't yet have an equivalent test for EQ to that for IQ, but we can roughly chart and evaluate our emotional age. The process of emotional growth has a timetable that is allied to the development of our cognitive faculties and our brain and biological formation. We expect occasional tantrums from a young child but wouldn't anticipate them from a 45-year-old executive—or would we? The individual's identity may learn to control, cover up, or even suppress the expression of such emotions while not necessarily developing or maturing them. Why would the identity want to?

Classically, therapy has focused on two methods of managing our emotions: cognitive and appraisal.

The cognitive method requires us to think about the emotion we want to work on and by doing so, to try to temper our reactions to the stimulus that causes the emotions to express themselves in action. The sequence that has been identified runs from stimulus to appraisal to action tendency to feeling. What is crucial in making any cognitive intervention is the length of time for which we can prolong the appraisal process. The longer we can extend this period, the less likely we are to act and then feel instant regret. This is a fascinating study, but not the focus of this book.

The second method is to evoke the feelings of the emotion and appraise them. This involves training that allows us to manage the emotion (very much the focus of psychotherapy) and establish control over it by our cognitive faculties working on the stimulus.

The classical options for managing our emotional life are either to work from our IQ or to work by evoking our EQ and exercise our cognitive faculties on the process. I would suggest there is a third way that is more rigorous and more demanding but infinitely more enhancing. To explore why we have the emotions we have, seek to separate out the identity that uses adolescent emotions to continue its role as hostage keeper, and choose our emotional responses brings emotional maturity and growth beyond anything that the two other methods can achieve.

Take an emotional pattern common in all infants, the search for instant gratification of needs. In early life when we are hungry we cry, when we want attention we may make any number of noises. As children mature we notice that the time between the need arising and the demand for its gratification can be prolonged. Studies have shown conclusively that where children are able to delay their demand for instant gratification, they later have much greater success in the workplace at higher executive levels. So far, this is very reasonable. After all, many strategies for working with people require us to hold our tongue, to wait for the right moment to confront an issue, and so forth.

However, this pattern of delaying gratification can be developed to a new level with our SQ intelligence. Ask yourself why you get angry, have demands, expect others to comply, and so on. Such an exploration will quickly reveal that it is again our identity that makes these demands. The more we have these needs, the less developed is the core of our self. The demands of our identity extend to the need to be recognized, to be thought to be intelligent, smart, successful, beautiful, and clever. However, when we make even a cursory analysis of these needs, it becomes obvious that they serve mostly to sustain and even grow the identity and help us little to engage with any higher realms of intelligence. Given the choice, who would really want to be thought of as clever, successful, and smart at the expense of actually feeling useful, whole, happy, and enhanced?

The SQ process does not calculate what we give and what we can then expect back in return based on our short-term or long-term emotional and mental investments. Emotions become enhanced inner feelings when guided by the SQ process, which elevates our life to new levels of satisfaction, interest, and curiosity—in the now. Meaning is life's own reward.

Evolutionary psychologists would make the case that by deferring today's pleasures for tomorrow's rewards, we enable a new range of opportunities and skills. We can plan ahead, store food, and make journeys further and further afield to explore more distant territories, thus increasing our capability and freedom. But spiritual intelligence doesn't try to extend this pattern of independence by delaying gratification; it tries to overcome the need to be gratified altogether. SQ individuals are thankful for the opportunity of living and see their response as the meaningful development of their SQ inner core. They are always "at home" in themselves.

Self-sabotage

Neuroscientist Joseph Le Doux writes:

> *Take the power of emotions to disrupt thinking itself. Neuroscientists use the term "working memory" for the capacity of attention that holds in mind the facts essential for completing a given task or problem, whether it be the ideal features one seeks in a house while touring several prospects or the elements of a reasoning problem on a test. The prefrontal cortex is the brain region responsible for working memory. But circuits from the limbic brain to the prefrontal lobes mean that the signals of strong emotion—anxiety, anger and the like—can create neural static, sabotaging the ability of the prefrontal lobe to manage working memory. That is why when we are emotionally upset, we say we just "can't think straight" and why continued emotional distress can create deficits in a child's intellectual abilities.*

The stress of fitting the bigger truth into a small space has devastating consequences. I would suggest that what Le Doux describes as a kind of "sabotaging" by the emotions can be fundamentally overcome by developing an SQ level of self. SQ is meaning first. It sets the contexts of living.

In his book *Emotional Intelligence*, Daniel Goleman calls this sabotaging process "emotional hijacking." We are triggered into anger or rage quite against the reasoning we would normally apply to a situation. While Goleman chronicles some extreme cases, crimes of passion, rage, and violent behavior, in my view this process is happening all the time. By expecting gratification, whether it be respect from employees, love from one's spouse, or adoration from one's children, we are loading the conditions in which this emotional hijacking is more liable to happen. We are empowering our identity to sabotage our deeper intelligence's motive to grow.

Creating a continual inner dialog that projects how wonderful, important, or even perfect our life is, accompanying it with happy smiles and contrived behavior, sets up an inevitable context for emotional hijacking. Ensuring that others speak their lines on cue to the inner script we create is a notoriously tricky business.

The seven levels of deenveloping identity

If we have based our self around self-proving identities of how clever, successful, or happy we are, we are bound to come into conflict with anything or anyone that implicitly or explicitly challenges this assumed truth. The skill of spiritual intelligence is to be what is needed today, what is meaningful in this particular situation, and not to become identified with our last success or previous achievements. Always start afresh with the situation we are in.

We cannot own intelligence, we need to find it. Higher intelligence is generated afresh each day and this allows us to understand the truth of our situation each day and each moment. Warming up an old intelligence formula to feed this or that situation is a feast of cold comfort.

The identity can be seen as having seven levels. While it is inevitable that we have an identity, when we lose touch with our SQ core and the identity takes over at the expense of the growth of our real self, it can take much effort and experiment to find it again. Identity is useful as an expression that we can adopt to suit the occasion, it is the clothing of emotional appropriateness, but this can never be the core or foundation for what we do.

Meaning develops as our spiritual intelligence deenvelops the influence of our previous level of identity and attunes us to a new and higher level of self. These seven levels describe patterns of behavior and thinking that span the different levels of life, from a very small and enclosed identity life (level 1) to a life that is ever searching and engaged in the greater meanings of why we do what we do (levels 5 and above).

Level 1—This person considers mainly the gratification of their desires, hungers, appetites. "I am hungry, need money, feel irritated, am at work and fed up, in a marriage that I want out of." This level of complaint can overwhelm us into basing our view of our situation, and our responses to it, almost entirely in local and short-term exigencies. We always want to be doing something different to what we are, to be somewhere different to where we are. The identity wants to recruit others to its cause to validate itself.

Level 2—This person considers the physical situation. "I am in a room, in my car, in bed, I am married, have three kids, have a job. I am a manager, a bookkeeper, a schoolteacher. I live at number 19 in this or that street." This is more neutral, less based in temporary emotional reactions than level 1. At this level we think in platitudes and not truths and say things such as "Life is not all bad," "You can't win them all," "You have to take the good with the bad." Life runs on by chance and mood. Like tabloid newspapers, it describes everything in terms of opinions.

Level 3—This will be about the processes we have going on in us at any moment. "I am generally happy, a bit unclear where my life is going, unfulfilled in my purpose. I am developing a better life style, am losing weight, am studying to improve myself. I love my family and want to give them a good life. I can't complain, could be better but could be a lot worse." This is the beginning of the development of character, doing the decent thing, trying to be settled with our self while seeking ways to improve, although still within a limited "my world" perception..

Level 4—This is about certainties and uncertainties. "My family life is settled, my children are at a good school, I am respected by my peers, I do a good day's work and am thinking about a career path that will allow me to improve our stability and standard of life. But I feel that something more is possible, and wonder what it might be." The dissatisfaction with our level is a quality of honesty of self and indicates an openness to grow further. It seeks dialog and explores openly. It is to know that we are empty and cease to cover up.

Level 5—This is about our situation viewed from a bigger picture than just the context of local community and domestic affairs. From this level, the individual considers the greater truth of the situation and how this greater truth oppresses us to find a deeper core to act from. Building higher qualities of character features here, for example needing to feel honorable. At this level, we cannot avoid exercising choice except by practicing self-deception.

Level 6—This is about greater purposes than purely personal considerations. "I have a certain number of years to do what I see is important. I am conscious of why I do what I do and want only to work for these ends."

Level 7—These individuals know what they want to do with their lives and are settled and committed to serving that greater purpose. Each day they find new intelligence to review the challenges of life and their life is expressed as a mission to which they are content to be of service.

St. Francis of Assisi was gardening one day and was asked by a student what he would do if he knew that this would be his last day on earth. "Why, finish the garden," he replied. SQ individuals express their core through everyday activities that others might view as mundane.

You might want to ask yourself which of the seven levels you see yourself living the majority of your life. When you have done this, look to the level above it. Ask yourself whether you are able to listen and attune yourself to the level above. Are you aware that it is perhaps filtering into your awareness? How can you encourage this level—what do you need to do to begin that change?

Awareness and reaction

If we take some examples of daily awareness, we can see more clearly how our reactive self cuts us off from the opportunity to grow into a new and higher level of meaning.

Awareness	Reactive self
The phone rings	We answer it
Someone gets angry	We argue with them or try to pacify them
A car horn sounds	We shout back
The crowd pushes forward for the few seats on the train	We push back
The alarm clock rings	We get up
A deadline is missed	We panic
We lose our car keys	We start looking for them
Someone asks a question	We assume we know the answer and talk as if we do
We get a job as a leader	We assume a "leadership style"

When called on to explain why we do what we do, we attribute meaning to our acts a posteriori. Why did we answer the phone? Because it was ringing. Why did we argue? Because the other person was angry and shouting. Why did we shout at the person in the other car? Because they were honking at us, how dare they!

This develops to more complex reactions in the name of everything from leadership to love. Why did we delay answering someone's phone call? It showed them I am not available and therefore that I am busy and important as a person. Why do we love this person? Because they are my wife or husband.

We might act in a particular way as an expression of what we call leadership or being a spouse, but to be able to recognize this level of the reactive self is invaluable in keeping that level of intelligence from running our life. Becoming conscious that our adolescence is mostly role playing is the beginning of developing to adulthood.

To deenvelop ourselves from this reactive self is to be aware of it and choose to resist it until we can find a new meaning. This is not so easy. Struggle, even if for one day, not to act from your usual reactive self. Remember, meaning cannot be added on as an afterthought in living.

So resist answering the phone until you choose a reason to answer. Resist getting into arguments, discussions, or debates until you can find a "bigger picture" reason to do so. Resist reacting to a rude person until you can find a higher truth to act from.

Separating reactive self from core meaning

I have found the framework of the following diagrams (Figures 8 and 9) invaluable in helping me separate my identity from my inner SQ growth. You can apply your own examples, but let me demonstrate with a simple one.

I am leafing through a recent copy of *Newsweek* and the front cover catches my awareness, as it is meant to do. It headlines the increase of obesity in western countries. I turn to the article inside and read that new figures are emerging all the time about eating disorders, the effects of obesity on long-term health, and so on. In fact, 31 percent of Americans and 22 percent of British people are now officially obese.

We can plot our awareness of and reactions to this issue as follows.

Figure 8 describes how the issues that we are aware of in our identity, we react to and cut off from. We are not actually engaged in the truth of the situation.

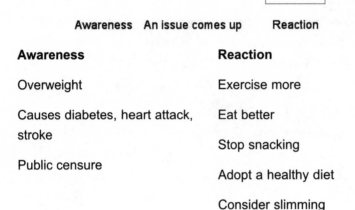

Awareness	Reaction
Overweight	Exercise more
Causes diabetes, heart attack, stroke	Eat better
	Stop snacking
Public censure	Adopt a healthy diet
	Consider slimming

Figure 8

Being informed about obesity, for example by reading a newspaper article, leads along a line of awareness of what obesity is and what might cause a reaction that alters our behavior.

However, being propelled from one thing to another, reaction after reaction, is meaningless. What we think of as choices are often nothing more than reactions to altering opinions that we become aware of within the confinement of our self-identity, ensuring that nothing really changes. That is the point. Inside this dualistic awareness–reaction mode the intelligence doesn't countenance change, it only alters pressures and shifts importance. We can claim that we want to do great things in the world, but in the absence of a new level of self this simply cannot happen.

The SQ model of intelligence reveals a third path that, in this example, countenances neither staying on the same diet nor reacting with a super-slimming regime.

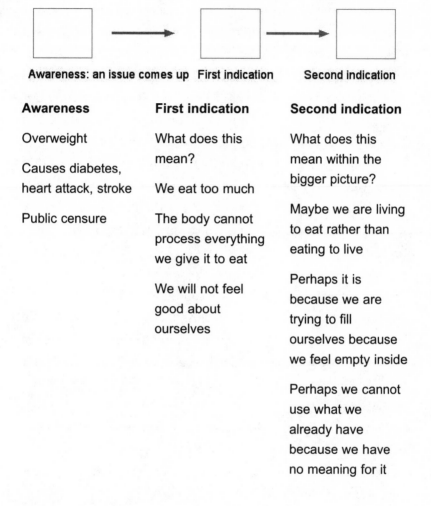

Awareness	First indication	Second indication
Overweight	What does this mean?	What does this mean within the bigger picture?
Causes diabetes, heart attack, stroke	We eat too much	Maybe we are living to eat rather than eating to live
Public censure	The body cannot process everything we give it to eat	Perhaps it is because we are trying to fill ourselves because we feel empty inside
	We will not feel good about ourselves	Perhaps we cannot use what we already have because we have no meaning for it

Figure 9

As we can see, by developing our awareness through the three-intelligence model, the same example of obesity develops not just a reactive and personal meaning, but a meaning within a bigger picture (box three). In this third box we don't have specific answers but a field of inquiry. At root obesity is about some deeper existential issue and not some outer habit. Reacting to obesity with pills, eating less, or exercising more is not addressing the root causes. Reactions dismiss the space within, where the presence of our self can begin to grow a higher intelligence about its own life and the challenges it faces.

Train yourself to become aware of your awareness, in this case your awareness of obesity. Then move on to the second box and seek to understand the implications of obesity, rather than instantly looking for some quick fix to deal with it.

Again, resist reaction but then in box three, seek to understand what box two means within a bigger truth of the situation. This is where we will be able to catch the growth of meaning within the bigger picture. Bearing in mind that SQ is a live intelligence, we should not be looking for a single monolithic answer. We are searching for a way to develop a new level from which the significant problems that we face can be solved.

We resist the usual reaction/answer—"I'll diet," "I'll become healthier"—which addresses only the physical level of the issue, and we reframe the question to include the greater chain of being of our self and the bigger picture of the world we engage with.

Some of the meanings that reveal themselves in the bigger picture are not "answers" but stimulate deeper awareness that begins a search for further meanings, which then makes the connection to new levels of the bigger picture.

This is the beginning of a network of early awareness and meaning that promotes further searches and explorations. The actions we may take do not show themselves at this step. Reaction is premature and usually engages the same old intelligence level yet again. Going on a diet, doing some exercise, will not help change the situation. It may make for a thinner obese person.

We cannot just assume that things mean something. It's not intellectual or emotional reasons that are being sought in

Step Two, but real meanings. The outcome may look the same, but they do not have the same presence or intelligence about them.

For example, the dietitian who says "You must do what you feel is right" is passing the pressures back to the patient. In contrast, the dietitian who advises an obese person *not* to diet until they have found a good reason is trying to develop a meaningful space in which action and resolve can come as a choice.

As we shall see in the next step, Evaluation, the scope for growth is unending. Why we argue, why we use force to resolve conflicts, why we get stressed, issues of love, success, relationships, happiness, mission, parenthood, leadership—all these are trying to press themselves on our awareness every day. If we don't cut off from the presence of our self, we can find new directions and potentialities in living. What we can be fairly certain about is that all these issues do not, in the words of our Irish guide from Chapter 4, start from where we are.

DEENVELOPMENT EXERCISES

1   Don't just react to people and situations but pause and consider before you act. The longer you can hold the period between stimulus and reaction, the more you will be able to choose your responses in the future. These become your self-leadership ability to change the directions of conflicts, useless arguments, circuitous conversations, and so on.

2.   Disarm the enemy (the identity) in your self by whenever and wherever possible declaring your background mood. If you are angry or irritable, tell those you are dealing with that this is the case. This reduces the influence of your mood and lessens the likelihood that these background influences will hijack your behavior to do something you will later regret. Remember, what is unspoken speaks loudest!

3   Train yourself not to deal in attitudes of assumption and taking for granted—this cuts off the possibility of new engagement. Expect yourself to have to find ways to cause things to happen and win each situation afresh. This begins by being aware of the assumptions that we continually have but are not aware of. For example:

- ❏   Don't assume that you can go to sleep on an argument and wake up fresh.
- ❏   Don't assume that you can leave business unfinished and not have it bother you at some level.
- ❏   Don't assume that you can have the alarm clock wake you and not react with pressure (fight and flight).

DEVELOPMENT EXERCISES

1   Consider a situation to which you know you are likely to react and choose what positive attitude you intend to have instead. Then maintain that attitude consistently throughout the situation. This trains the mind to your chosen responses rather than you becoming a victim of your reactions. What is important is *not* to try to solve problems directly, but to build a growing interest in the whole field of knowledge surrounding the issue that you have perhaps not explored.

2   Changing your background moods requires extensive training, but you can begin by working out in advance why you want to act the way you do in any given situation by seeing what will be the consequences in the bigger picture. This will begin to influence your emotional and thinking responses. Just behaving "as if" you are happy or "as if" you are positive when you are not has limited usefulness and will not build new intelligence, but will mildly reconnect back to more positive states. Meaning requires that you actively and deliberately find a reason to engage that is self-chosen.

3   Practice the three-part template of thinking as shown in Step Two. This is highly effective in overcoming useless reactions that assume to understand and will also help develop new insights and perceptions. Mentally clear arguments before you sleep, finish unfinished business, and bring the reasons that you want to engage in a new day to mind before you sleep so that they are present when the alarm rings.

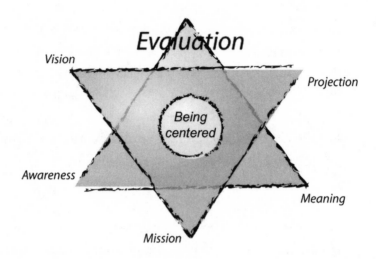

In Step Three we are going to look at how our way of making value judgments mostly arises from an inner sense of being disengaged from the core of SQ. We are accustomed to judging things according to fixed values, such as good or bad, likable or not, useful or not.

SQ evaluation is a living intelligence that seeks, quite literally, to come out of living values that allow growth, rather than assumed values that may be little more than attachments that have the effect of stifling growth.

When we evaluate in the SQ way, we are making assessments of where things are in their own growth inside the truth of the situation, from an inner sense that we too are growing within the truth of the situation.

7

Step Three: Evaluation

Man is not the creature of circumstances. Circumstances are the creatures of men.

Benjamin Disraeli

The great composer Wolfgang Amadeus Mozart and his wife are living way beyond their means in Vienna, the Austrian capital city of music. Wolfgang composes music during the day and goes partying at night. He has no head for economy. Frau Mozart knows that her husband produces golden eggs and, while she is concerned for the health of the golden goose, she is practical and wants to exact a good price for the eggs. After all, she is the one who pays the bills.

The film *Amadeus* shows how she decides on a course of action to alleviate their financial distress. She will take her husband's manuscripts to Antonio Salieri, the court composer and confidant to the Emperor, and ask his help to influence the Emperor favorably to give Mozart a new commission. Wolfgang would never dream of asking for favors. He expects the court to bow to his genius. Frau Mozart little suspects that the outwardly charming Antonio Salieri harbors a deep grudge against her husband, who threatens his position as the court's favorite composer.

Frau Mozart arrives at Salieri's chambers armed with some of her husband's latest manuscripts. At first Salieri stalls, asking her to come back later, but Frau Mozart refuses. As she explains, the manuscripts are all originals. Salieri cannot resist. He opens the portfolio and stands, transfixed, in the middle of his chambers, turning over page after page while each exquisite piece plays in his head. First a simple oboe playing a haunting melody, then an entire orchestra, then an opera, a symphony, a piano concerto... one masterpiece after another.

These originals are uncorrected, unchanged, first and only drafts. Mozart has simply written down music finished in his head, page after page of it, as if he were just taking dictation. And, as Salieri remarks, "Music finished as no music is ever finished... replace one note and there would be diminishment, replace one phrase and the structure would fall... here again was the very voice of God. I was staring through my cage at those meticulous brush strokes, at an absolute beauty."

The sublime music makes Salieri feel whole. It connects the great chain of being in him. His SQ core, his emotional intelligence, and his IQ are in those moments in harmony, as they were in his childhood years when he first loved music. His identity is temporarily displaced—he feels uplifted, almost free.

Frau Mozart watches Salieri, aware only of whether his face betrays a willingness to help, which would mean money.

"Is it not good?" she asks.

"It is miraculous," Salieri replies.

"Then you will help us?" Frau Mozart assumes.

With a grimace, Salieri leaves the room.

He feels whole when he hears beautiful music and yet he reacts to the terrible fact that it is not *him* who has created the music. He judges, from his cage, that the music will reduce his own fame and favor. One senses that if Salieri were not so possessed of his own self-importance, his jealous court composer identity could release him, to make music that would shine that much greater. His inner value of self has not yet chosen to affirm the opportunity of a higher self and the intelligence of his outer identity runs contrary to his natural inner intelligence

He finally resolves to kill Mozart rather than suffer the contradiction of loving his music and hating the God that didn't endow him with the same genius. In the absence of a clear self-chosen value at his core, he will kill what he loves the most—because he cannot possess it for himself.

Salieri is a good example of the divided self, as R. D. Laing called it. This highlights a difficulty that we all face, a contradiction that we struggle with—the more we aspire to greatness, the more the occupying identity that covers over our genius core stirs in antagonism at the pure, volatile, and free SQ response. The identity, though it loves to talk of freedom, do great things, make a difference, is not free and curses any who are. It is in just such moments of judgment that we curse and imprison our higher levels of self.

Greatness is above all else the liberation of self. "I want to make a difference in this world," "I want to be the best I can be," "I want to make my mark." These are all aspirations we hear voiced at every level of society and in every sphere, but there is a large gap between assuming that we can and knowing that we are able. We may talk and we may walk, but the neural pathways (if there are any) connecting the talk to the walk may well be absent.

What do you value?

For a moment, think about the things you value and imagine for the purposes of this exercise that they might actually not be important. I'm not asking you to try to devalue them, but just to consider, as difficult as it may be, that what you assume to be valuable might not be.

People I have asked to do this exercise often say, "Of course I value my family or my kids or my career" and are indignant that anyone should suggest otherwise. Let me offer an example from my own life to illustrate this contradiction.

"I love and value my wife" is something I say and think and it has a sense of being a pervading feeling that covers everything. I reason to myself that if anyone saw us together they would think so too. It is not something I have to think about (a defense often made about emotions, which we will see later is ill founded). Of course, my love extends to wanting to look after her, provide for her, be there for her, and much more besides.

Some years ago she had a minor operation. When she came home from the hospital, I resolved to be the best help I could possibly be. I wanted to care for her and be there 24 hours a day until she was better. Barely an hour passed in which I didn't ask her how she was or if there was anything she needed.

For the first couple of days I went to bed each night with a glow of satisfaction that I had been the best help a partner could be. I plumped up pillows, aired the room, talked in a soft voice, and generally adopted a very convincing role. Her illness was the problem and I was firmly on the job of sorting it.

Where had I got this role from? A mixture of IQ and EQ models that my identity had gleaned from a range of life's experiences: television, my father doing the same for my mother, and a general impression that doing a lot of things for someone was helpful. Had I ever actually asked or checked to understand whether this was love or value in any bigger sense, or studied in myself (that is, in the bigger picture of my real self) what love actually is? No. But of course this was love—I am a loving person and I was acting out of love. Who could doubt it?

As the days went on I noticed that it became harder and harder to keep up this level of attention. By the fourth day I was begrudging the need to run downstairs for the umpteenth time to fetch something. Yet still I kept up the act.

"Is there anything you need, anything at all?" I heard myself asking, particularly when I experienced any resentment. I felt more and more like the hotel manager that John Cleese made famous in the television series *Fawlty Towers*. A broad grin covered a seething indignation that was ready to explode at any moment.

One evening, I sat down exhausted. I remember picking out a book that I thought might inspire me, a biography of Mother Teresa. But when I looked at the photograph of her, I saw none of the smiling emotional sympathy I had characterized in the previous days. Instead, I saw a face that was a little stern, of course with a deep core of love, but also with a very businesslike, get-to-it attitude.

I wrote my impressions of her in my diary later that evening. Mother Teresa's eyes seemed to be saying to all those she tended:

❖ "I will help you to help yourself, but you are responsible and I will not take that responsibility from you."

❖ "You will not have my sympathy, because that will connect you to what caused you to be ill, but you will have my support in equal measure to how you try to become well or face what you have to face."

❖ "Your strength is not in thinking about your illness but in thinking about why you want to live and grow and the value you have for life, no matter how long you are here for."

I had the terrible realization that my kind of "love and value" was at best a judgment of what I thought was needed from an assumed level of self, a self that hadn't even evaluated what real love was. All the issues I had written in my diary were ones that drew me into the bigger picture of understanding:

❖ I will help you to help yourself to recover but you are responsible—everyone has choice.

❖ You will not have my sympathy but you will have my support—it is each person's responsibility to reconnect to their core and the intelligence of emotional sympathy will not help.

❖ Your strength is in thinking about why you want to live—intelligent understanding of the truth of the situation is the way to reestablish that connection.

Love can either be an emotionally laced behavior that suggests meaning or it can bring a person closer to the truth of their situation. To love someone is to want them to succeed in what is real and this may encourage them to grow into a level of self that even those closest to them may not know.

Love is not taking on someone else's problems, it is creating a situation in which they can accurately and successfully deal with them for themselves and grow beyond them. Love does not induce dependence but independence and in time interdependence, a higher level altogether.

Some time later, when my wife was better, I asked her whether she had felt moments when I had been a touch irritable or even resentful about her being ill.

"Oh yes," she said, as if I had asked her whether she had noticed a bear had walked into the room.

"Why didn't you say so?" I asked.

"I knew you were doing your best to help me and I didn't want to complain." Then with a smile she added, "And I was too ill to take care of you as well as myself!"

Evaluation is always from a bigger picture

When spiritual energy is directed on something outward, then it is a thought. The relation between it and you first makes you, the value of you, apparent.

Ralph Waldo Emerson

Evaluation is a release from judgment and an elevation into the perceptions that come from a bigger picture. It's a little like those bottles of aspirins with child-proof lids. To open the bottle you need to push down the cap (inward action) and turn (outward action) at the same time. Evaluation requires an inward and an outward act.

The process of evaluation should never be undertaken from the identity level of self. We should only evaluate from a bigger picture, else we will suffer the same kind of contradictions and conflicts as Salieri. What we say we value outwardly requires of us a searching attitude to find new values, new feelings, new appreciations to keep that value alive. To love ourselves or other people is to love what a life can become, not just how we or they serve the confined limitations of our identity of self. Nowhere is this clearer to see than when a partner changes and becomes different to the person we say we love.

Our inability to come to terms with this one step alone accounts for much of the stress and distress we suffer every day. We are one thing on the outside and something else on the inside. What we say we want and value and what we actually are forge a contradictory relationship and trying to "manage" the difference becomes a daily preoccupation. The good manager of self can continually make the books add up, income and out-going, but the good leader of self is able to find new opportunities, new resources, in a third intelligence. This step marks the difference between managing self and leading self.

If I say that I value my colleagues at work, I need to see what that means in the bigger picture. Do I mean that I value them only for what they do for me or that I value them in the whole of what they are and what they may become? They may in time surpass my own abilities and become my boss. Would I value them then? This second meaning in the bigger picture is likely to rub my identity up the wrong way.

To want another person to succeed in all they are and can become (Figures 2 and 3) implies that we value their opportunity to grow and evolve as individual and unique selves. When we examine the identity that says "I want only the best for others" and "I want all to reach their true potential," that is easier said than done. It brings us into conflict with our self-identity.

To really value another is to have affirmed the self-value that our own life is an opportunity to grow a new core (again, Figures 2 and 3). Real value flows from affirming our own self-value at core; inversely, the more we exercise judgment on others, the more we confirm our self-identity and prevent any new perception from any new level of self.

Evaluation tries to understand our self and to understand the other person. The situation *everyone* faces is that we are locked out of the meaning-giving core and are trying to find a way to make sense of our life. To fix others from a fixed self-identity is to keep the door very much closed on being able to resource the SQ intelligence. Of all the steps, this is perhaps the most difficult to see precisely because we are divided selves. We act as if we have the best interests of others at heart, while covering up any challenge to our self-identity.

"I really tried," a friend told me about his relationship. "No one could fault me on that. I just couldn't save our marriage." That's an incomplete statement. Did he try wisely? Did he try according to his fixed view of what trying requires? Did he evaluate the truth of the situation or simply judge the other person? The idea that because we invest time and effort we are vindicated is the cause of a great deal of conflict.

Step three requires what we colloquially call an open mind or a whole mind. To listen to another person without judging or exercising our opinion on them is difficult—it requires self-knowledge. And self-knowledge is understanding that as long as we are different outwardly to how we are inwardly, we will only extend those imbalances to others.

Overcoming the division of self

When we judge others, we judge ourselves. If we could understand the truth of the situation it would make us free, but we judge the truth and edit out those parts that don't fit with how the script of our life should run. We would be free by being at another level, the level of SQ, and real understanding would show us that what we have become would rather kill the golden goose than face the truth.

To understand the truth of the situation *as it is* is to recognize the fundamental need for a change.

When we judge others from the confines of our own "box" (Figure 6), we can only make comparisons of how much better "I am" or how much worse "they are." We fail to understand the bigger picture in which everyone faces the same fundamental issues (Figure 7).

The division mentality

The managing director of a medium-sized company recently consulted me about the difficulties he was having with his staff. He is a likable man, in his late 50s, is self-made, and now works less and tries to enjoy the fruits of his labor: golf at weekends, long holidays, and a house that is the envy of many. But he can't quite leave his work. The same old challenges come back to cloud his mind again and again.

"You know, Richard, I can't tell you how hard I've tried in all these years, but no matter what I do, the guys here just don't work as a team. They always seem to be divided; no one really communicates with anyone else.

"I give them good wages, good working conditions, I truly value them—what else do they want? You just can't seem to please anyone these days. I know what it is to have built this company, they have it easy. I want us all to pull together as a team, but I can't make it happen. What do you think we can do?"

I call this the division mentality. It can't understand the situation and expresses values against expected returns:

❖ I have tried so hard, therefore there should be a good result.

❖ I have given my husband everything he needs, I don't understand why he isn't happy.

❖ I love my children, so why don't they behave and show me respect?

There is an assumption that "I" is one and the same person who has "tried so hard" and then expects a "good result," but looking more closely this is not the case. This book is underpinned by the notion that we are a divided self until we choose to reoccupy our core. We have an SQ core that is covered over by a continually altering identity whose intelligence makes sure that we *do not* understand the truth of the situation. We are a broken chain that sees all kinds of issues "out there," but cannot understand that there is only one issue we ever face "in here," the chosen return to a wholeness at a new level of self. Only from this wholeness can we develop an integrated way of thinking.

The division mentality is visible in families, work situations, schools, teams, and of course in ourselves. The first and most important task is to understand it before we act.

Figure 10 describes how division makes for more and more fragmentation and cannot lead to any real unity.

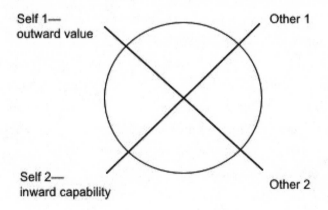

Figure 10 The division mentality

Let's begin with our MD's statement. He talks outwardly about a team and his value for the team. He then assumes inwardly that this value is real and intact in himself and he is capable of delivering the same knowledge to himself—but he is not a team. He sees that his staff are not a team and he is trying to find the intelligence with which to build a team, but this can only be found by integrating his own duality.

He is aware of "teamship" in the wrong way with the wrong sense, too fight and flight based, alert to the aspects of staff's behavior that are not like a team as he expects and judges it to be. His focus is on how this person doesn't get on with that person, how this person doesn't appreciate how much the boss values them, and so on.

So from the frustration of there not being a team, the MD shifts to consider why he thinks there should be a team: "I give them good wages, good working conditions, I truly value them—what else do they want?" This is how the alteration of states goes on at the same level, with no elevation to a new level of self.

❖ MD Self 1 says: "I built the company, I have employed these people, I pay them, but they don't communicate" (observational, more IQ based).

❖ MD Self 2 says: "I want us all to pull together and be responsible for the company as a team" (emotionally immature and fluctuating between hope and frustration, assuming that this can make a difference).

These two divided aspects of self replicate themselves in the staff, who think:

❖ Staff Self 1: "We are part of the same company—we can make decisions, work out what is best in a collaborative way" (emotional pleading, dependent and assumed values).

❖ Staff Self 2: "He is making all the decisions and all he does is complain! I will leave it up to him—my views are not heard anyway" (withdrawing to a cool IQ analysis by using emotional strategies that seek to punish and distance the boss).

MD Self 1 causes reactions in Staff Self 2. Staff Self 2 then retreats from participation, which enrages MD Self 2 so that he wants to include others.

MD Self 2 thus tries to do this, which allows Staff Self 1 to take the initiative. This causes MD Self 1 to reclaim the territory: "I build the company, don't they realize it is all on my head if it fails."

The truth of the situation cannot be understood by a divided self that judges what is wrong from its own level while wanting something higher and better. We need to find a way to integrate Self 1 and Self 2 in a higher, integrated process before we start demanding that others are a team. That process needs to begin in the MD, who is himself a divided player.

When I explained this to the MD, it was interesting how the dialog developed. He told me why he had started the business, a natural medicine company. His mother had been ill with cancer and was told by the hospital that nothing could be done to help her. The MD simply would not accept this and after an initial period of apathy and devastation, resolved that there must be something that could be done. He made contact with an Ayurvedic doctor who had also been trained in traditional medicine and a number of other fields of complementary medicine. As a result of that doctor's intervention, the MD's mother lived for another seven years with a remarkably good quality of life.

"One day it struck me," he said, "that if we always accept that nothing can be done, nothing will be done. I had almost accepted the hospital's view. When I looked back on the experience, I felt as if I had broken free. I was going to live according to the principle that much *can* be done."

It was clear that this experience had caused a deep sense of unity in him and it was from that sense of unity that his great achievements had flourished. However, in building a business he had drifted back to his identity, valuing making profits and being successful more than the love of what could be done. He had supplanted the value of personal growth with the value of gold and quiet weekends in the garden, and was back in the realm of what couldn't be done. He longed not for more success but to reclaim what he had lost on his journey to success.

The triune of understanding

Step three completes the first triune of the seven steps, the triune of understanding. Before we act, we need to understand. This requires not just an IQ level, nor just an EQ process, but a triune of intelligences that understand the truth of the situation. Whether we are on a plane, in a boardroom, at the beach, by ourselves, with our family, we can know ourselves by standing under the truth of the situation. Trying to stand *over* the truth of the situation is assumed identity thinking.

I remember attending a presentation skills session many years ago. I was impressed by the trainer, who was working with a woman who felt very uncomfortable giving a speech without notes. Her body language and the tension in her voice seemed to say "I am incomplete without my notes," which con-tradicted the fact that she was showing others how to make presentations.

At a certain point the trainer turned to her and said quite firmly: "Haven't you trained yourself to trust your inner systems yet?" This was an immediate awakening in her of the meaning of the association between a person and their inner systems. Our inner systems are incredibly accurate, can recognize a face in a crowd, can recollect the smallest details, and can spot an inaccuracy from a whole field of text. The trainer had obviously seen how the woman was judging herself by self-limiting what she was telling herself could not be done, while telling others what could be done.

What impressed me was the accuracy of the statement from an SQ standpoint; so different from a command such as "Do it without notes" or the emotional sympathy of pleading "It's all right; you can do it without your notes." "Haven't you trained yourself to trust your inner systems yet?" focused on the woman's divided self. Deal with this and it was possible to build on her natural communication skills. Fail to do so and she would be forced to learn ever more complex techniques to cover the basic insecurity of her identity.

Over the years I have learnt never to use notes for even a whole day presentation. If I am not making my own fresh search for new intelligence, all I am doing is telling people about SQ rather than acting from my value of the opportunity to engage with it. Perhaps the biggest struggle I faced in developing from an intensely shy individual to someone who can address large audiences without notes was my self-judgment, having been trained at school to have a fixed IQ value about myself and to judge myself in relation to others. Being brave and believing in the value of the core intelligence cannot be surpassed—it is not designed to impress others, it is a level of consciousness that serves to benefit all.

The following table contains examples of the three intelligences in language. Where our language lacks a word, I have suggested one in italics.

IQ	EQ	SQ
Reactive	Proactive	*Coactive*
Dependent	Independent	Interdependent
Devolve	Resolve	Evolve
Possess	Process	*Cocess*
Detract	Retract	Contract
Depress	Impress	Express
Division	Revision	Vision
Expire	Respire	Inspire
Reflective	Selective	Collective
Absolve	Resolve	Solve
Monological	Dialogical	*Translogical* or *trilogical*

The first column is about the dependent individual who seeks to get for themselves (possess) and is divisive, reactive, by so being.

The second column is about process, having individual thoughts, feelings, processes, coming to our own views, becoming independent, not having to rely on everyone and everything else, thinking and feeling for ourselves.

Column three is the level of SQ. Scattered throughout our language are examples that suggest a higher-level state of affairs that carries unity, coexistence, interdependence, inspired vision, and solving problems by being joined to that new level.

We can all cite examples of how the "team" is greater than the players, but if the team is only an emotional idea, without any new sustained level of intelligence, then individualism will very quickly divide it again at the first signs of difficulty. A real team does not need everyone to agree or even seem harmonious, but does require that the fundamental understanding of the truth of the situation is the same in everyone.

The first triune of awareness, meaning, and evaluation reestablishes the great chain of being. Understanding, the sum of the first three steps, is essentially holistic. It connects our self up as a cognitive feeling and knowing inner self and it reconnects the outer world up into chains of meaning that we have largely learnt to reduce to a materialistic flatland of issues and ideas that do not even awaken an interest to search and understand.

By relying too heavily on IQ information, we break the natural harmonies of sequence that link principles with processes and with hard information. Meaning is lost in the equation of IQ-based thinking. In the end we will need brain science to show us that it is good to clean our teeth at night.

Our spiritual intelligence would have us wonder about the way life works, asking why and delving deep into the intelligence of life. SQ is an integrating intelligence that links all the parts together.

From understanding the truth of the situation we turn in the next chapter to centering our self in the higher truth.

DEENVELOPMENT EXERCISES

1   Don't judge others in terms of right and wrong or good and
    bad according to your assumptions, but find out the reason
    they do what they do. Ask them, if you can. Apply the same
    evaluation principle to yourself. This is never accomplished
    by exerting pressure and blame but is done with a genuine
    interest in understanding the reasons for things—you will be
    surprised.

2   Don't let your posture be reactive to irritations. Become
    watchful about what causes you to change posture and
    why—it can condition the three intelligences from the outside
    to the inside, which confines the self. Posture reflects bal-
    ances and pressures and training yourself to handle pressure
    with ease for even short periods, even seconds, will increase
    the window of opportunity to choose other responses than the
    usual ones. As an example, if argument causes you to get
    close and confrontational or to back off, explore what oppor-
    tunities there are in the middle ground.

3   Don't assume you know how you were received in any situa-
    tion. Ask for reflections and feedback and listen in the SQ
    way—not just to the words that people say but what these
    cause in you. This allows you to get to know your identity's
    objections to change. Accept what people say and try to
    understand it—don't react!

DEVELOPMENT EXERCISES

1   Learning goes on throughout your life—if you don't separate life and learning. The world is a classroom. Make evaluations of what works and what doesn't and try to discover the principle behind why things do and don't work—this will be useful in becoming more conscious in your actions later. For example:

❑   Why does listening reduce the heat in someone's anger?

❑   Why does stepping back instill confidence in another person's attempt to express themselves?

❑   Why did fixing broken windows in New York have such an effect in reducing crime (see later in the book)?

2   Become a continual student of posture, voice, and speech in yourself and others. Get to know how posture conditions what can and cannot happen—and why. This allows you to develop the conscious use of posture—not just the outer act but the inner reason it works the way it does (from mind to body). As an example, if you find yourself becoming overly judgmental, try to finely balance the pressure of your middle fingers against your thumbs so that each hand is exactly the same—this will balance out the two hemispheres of the brain and reduce the tendency to judge.

3   Practice using language carefully and artfully. Don't always use the same evaluation phrases, like "that was great, cool, brilliant." Find exact words, metaphors, and similes to express the truth of what you have seen or heard or felt. Remember that the first person who listens to what you say is you and that accurate evaluation is a herald of being centered.

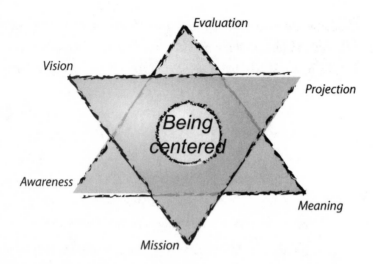

We are now going to look at a much-discussed concept: what does it mean to be centered in ourselves?

We often hear the term centered being used to describe some middle point in work–life balance from which we can cope and remain in balance. We perceive that center point as being between these "good" things on the one hand and those "bad" things on the other.

While the previous steps have caused us to be aware of our spiritual intelligence, its meaning, and its values, it is in Step Four that we come to see that the SQ sense of self is drawn from being centered in the truth of the situation. It is a less personal sense of self that carries a far greater sense of being part of something greater. When we are centered in what is really important, in growing what is of real value, we enable everyone to win.

8

Step Four: Being Centered

Ask and you shall be given, seek and you shall find, knock and the
door shall be opened unto you.
Matthew 9

I t is a few months before the outbreak of the Second World
War. Oskar Schindler is preparing himself for difficult times
the only way he knows how—by doing business. He is a
German industrialist, a womanizer, and a bon vivant—he is also
a member of the Nazi party. It helps to have good contacts, he
reasons. His business doesn't make him a fortune but it suffices
to sustain his lifestyle, a wife, and several mistresses. He is always
on the look out for new deals, new offers, and new ways to
expand his territory.

By 1939, the war has created new opportunities at the
expense of the local Jewish population, who are dispossessed of
property, rights, and business ownership. Schindler is able to pick
up some good businesses at knockdown prices. This is not a time
to question one's motives too carefully, it is a time to look after
one's own interests, keep one's nose clean, and survive.

By 1941, in Stephen Spielberg's film *Schindler's List*, we
see Schindler enjoying the fruits of his new business acquisitions.

He and his mistress are out for an afternoon of leisure, riding around the countryside around the old city. The sound of shooting from the city below draws them to a hilltop overlooking the newly created Jewish ghetto, a place of, as it is euphemistically called, "protection" for the local Jewish population. Uniformed German soldiers are systematically liquidating the ghetto, firing on civilians and killing or removing them section by section from their homes. At this rate, the German commander coldly calculates, the job will be completed by nightfall—the implication being that as long as the Jewish inhabitants don't create any problems, things will go swimmingly. And the best way the Jews can help is to be herded out of their homes or be killed with no resistance or fuss.

German music blares over the loud speakers to inspire the soldiers to the task, but it seems as if they need little encouragement. In the film, the juxtaposition of Strauss waltzes and the lively way the soldiers are going about their business would seem comical if one didn't look too closely at the meaning within the activity.

Schindler is unable to tear his eyes away. One senses that at this moment his life changes. What he had thought was a bad situation has now become an intolerable one.

In his book *Schindler's Ark*, on which the film is based, Thomas Keneally writes:

> *Oskar would lay special weight upon this day. "Beyond this day," he would claim, "no thinking person could fail to see what would happen. I was now resolved to do everything in my power to defeat the system."*

When we next see Schindler fraternizing with his Nazi "comrades," nothing appears altered and yet everything has changed.

Oskar remains a womanizer, a businessman, a member of the Nazi party, even a bon vivant who can hold his drink and party all night with high-ranking officials. He is astutely looking for new business opportunities—but all now for a new reason. He is going to use his outer persona, his identity, for a new inner principle. Any scruples he might have first had about profiting from the situation have vanished, completely and utterly. He is going to profit to the fullest measure and use the profit in every way to "defeat the system."

In all, Oskar Schindler has been credited with saving the lives of more than 1,600 Jewish people over a three-year period. He is honored in the Department of the Testimonies of the Yad Vashem in Jerusalem. To many he was not just their savior, a father figure, and a protector, but a center of sanity around which their most basic hope to be allowed to live could find an orbit.

Oskar Schindler became centered in a higher truth. He could tolerate others losing when he was centered only in his business, or having a hard time while he was profiting at their expense, but when the basic right of an individual to exist ceased to have meaning in the outer world, he was thrust into having to take a stance about life that he had never before consciously considered.

SQ centers self in a higher truth

My neighbor goes to yoga classes to "center" herself. When I asked her how she does this, she explained it this way:

I connect to the rhythmic motion of my breathing, my "Chi," and try to relax and let the pressures of the day evaporate. On the out breath

I release all my tensions and on the in breath I take in new life and
new energy. I slow down and center myself—it feels wonderful.

I have no doubt it does, but is this really being centered?
Look again at Figure 3, repeated below.

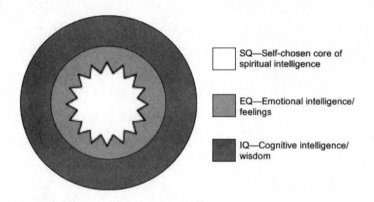

SQ—Self-chosen core of
spiritual intelligence

EQ—Emotional intelligence/
feelings

IQ—Cognitive intelligence/
wisdom

If steps one, two, and three bring us to understand the
truth of the situation, step four firmly centers our self at its core.
To be centered is to make the center of our self the bigger picture, and this can only be done by choosing to occupy our core
with that reason.

In Step Four, we will be looking at how at this point we
become whole, become an individual committed to the growth
of self as a meaningful life. The SQ individual expands their
inner intelligence from within to the world beyond.

When we talk of centering ourselves, we often mistakenly
think we are getting back into some balanced state (drawing our
reference from some out-of-balance state). We conceive of balance as some middle point away from all the stress, worry, tension, work, responsibilities... We see this point of balance as
some centrifuge that our movements revolve around, much in
the same way as when we walk along a tightrope with arms out-
stretched, we conceive balance as being between this point on

our left as we turn toward one arm and this point on our right as we turn toward the other.

As we "balance" the endless divisions of life and work, family and personal, the individual and the community, our perception is drawn, often wrongly, to how they are protagonists, each robbing the other of time and space. If I stay longer at work, I am damaging my family life, but if I stay at home I am abandoning the chance of advancing my career. Finding a peaceful coexistence between both sides, boss and spouse, can become like negotiating a peace between warring parties. In fact, it is often at explosive moments when we can no longer tolerate the stretching demands that the nature of this inner conflict emerges into the light of day: "I work hard for the family to give you a decent standard of living" or "This job has cost me my relationship."

Finding a center between the two, managing the two sides, does often mean occupying a middle point, an identity that achieves nothing more than survive the demands of each while keeping them apart. In this sense, my neighbor excels. She finds relaxation by relieving the conflict. This endless battle is the inevitable result of the indoctrination of a dualistic intelligence.

If there is one psychological and emotional feature that needs deenveloping in Step Four it is the ability to forgive ourselves, to let go of our self-developed guilt that we are letting someone down.

In SQ, being centered is to occupy a higher level of engagement altogether. It is only by releasing ourselves from what seems an impossible balancing act that we can elevate our level of self. The stress that many feel at the end of a day can be summed up by the words "I just haven't got any more to give." Try as we might, as much as we ask for understanding, tolerance, or help, as much as we seek to find time to satisfy all parties, there never seems enough to go round.

It is the act of a strong person to acknowledge that they can do no more as they are and that only inner change has access to more. The SQ individual allows the identity to become sublimated to a greater purpose—to serve a new level of self. As we see in Schindler's case, lying itself is not wrong, it is the reason we lie that makes it right or wrong.

We could say that it is only the level of intelligence of our self that prevents our entry to the core. It is by the admission of our self to our self that we can enter. When Schindler was forced to recognize that his life was a complete lie rather than a mild deceit, he had access to a new "why" in which to center himself.

The task of engagement

Centering ourselves does not mean withdrawing from life, engaging our ancient "reptilian" behavior, breathing slowly, sitting quietly, disengaged from the world, as my neighbor advocates. It is also beyond some middle point between our fight and flight mechanisms that can be the stuff of our daily reactions. It is both and neither. It is an engagement in the truth of our situation that is physiologically more like what we often refer to as a state of "flow," both quiet and intense.

Now it seems that science is focusing on a third neural circuit beyond the reptilian (freezing and immobility) and the mammalian (fight and flight) strategies. This has open-ended and far-reaching implications for human behavior across a broad range of territories. Is it possible, as an example, that we don't have to become stressed to be effective?

Dr. Stephen Porges of the University of Illinois in Chicago proposes a third level of the autonomic nervous system, a level of "social engagement," as he calls it in *Polyvagal Theory*. While fight and flight behaviors involve the two extremes of close physical confrontation in fight or distancing from danger in flight, he identifies a whole set of "in between" states that can be discerned in our social behavior and support a more highly evolved level of our nervous system.

When nursing or in reproduction, the formation of strong pair bonds requires immobilization. We mostly associate immobilization with the reptile's response to danger—it lays still, barely breathing, and in some cases even feigns death. But humans can develop close bonds without fear, a safe state that can only be accomplished by this third, "higher" level of the nervous system co-opting the neural circuits for immobilization.

Our nervous system is equipped to unconsciously register and evaluate risk in the environment and to adapt behavior accordingly. In the engaged state, intimacy becomes possible and meaningful by virtue of the complex language of social cues that make the situation "safe." Making eye contact, softness in the voice, smiling—these cues are regulated by direct pathways from the cortex to the brain stem that control the nerves that in turn control the muscles of the face and head. It is these muscles that influence both the expression of and our receptivity to these social cues. Human exchange can be both intimate and safe or, to put it in terms of SQ, the development of higher intelligence develops new opportunities for engagement.

As we become released from "fight and flight" behaviors to survive, we will be able to turn our intelligence toward new challenges that have been previously handled by the "old" systems. The deliberate fostering of those calm states (through love or respect, care or genuine concern) makes it conceivable to address challenges that we have previously struggled with through new neural circuits, new behaviors, new "educated" pathways.

Consider as an example a parent correcting a child with no underlying sense of challenge or chastisement, and how the child could then safely absorb (in the SQ core) new meanings that would translate into more emotionally mature behavior. Under threat, the child would only engage those limbic responses that are part of the fight and flight system.

Porges' model of a third level of human reactivity is particularly fascinating in that it challenges the assumptions we have in some very fundamental areas of living.

Engagement is the real task we face. To establish a meaningful core of self, we must understand the truth of our situation (through awareness, meaning and evaluation) and become centered or engaged in that truth. It is, after all, a feature of the SQ individual that their engagement in life is both intense and calm. They are able to work long hours, maintain high degrees of concentration and alertness, not develop stressful biases of judgment and emotional imbalance, and not resort to threat and guile to win the day.

They can also handle conflict with something akin to love, intimacy, or care. I have worked with many people in highly responsible positions who handle huge amounts of stress and conflict. I have seen how a third kind of centered response to difficulty not only diffuses tension but enables all involved to step into a new relationship.

Imagine yourself in the heat of argument vacillating between walking out in indignation and moving forward with verbal or physical attack. Then imagine the other person mirroring this behavior, also at one moment threatening and at another about to flee. Picture yourself moving into a middle ground, quite close to the other person, and saying quietly with no malice or threat, looking straight at them, "Yes, I understand what you are saying and your right to your own view, though I may not agree with it." This has an amazing effect and cuts through all tensions.

This behavior signals a spiritually intelligent level of truth. It says, "I cannot be harmed when I am unified and centered in my principles and chosen path."

Rudolf Guiliani describes how, when he became mayor of New York, he was told that incoming visitors to the city were advised not to make eye contact with New Yorkers for fear of inviting confrontation. While this disengagement was probably good general advice against potential robbers and muggers, it hardly makes for a city that people are keen to visit. It is at best a "survivalist" skill. Survival depends on being able to distinguish friend from foe and in an environment that is potentially both friendly and threatening, the safe strategy is to assume that all are potentially foes until proven otherwise.

The evolution of new neural systems that co-opt the older fight and flight and immobilization defense systems to more benign purposes enables behavior to be adapted to a more socially engaged state. Not engaging carries its own penalties. It means accepting a life of no meaning—a basic survival.

The dangers of putting off an engagement in life remind me of the biblical story of the father who gave each of his three sons a sum of money before he went away on a journey. When he returned, the first son had invested the money and his father took back only the original sum, leaving the son with what he had made. He did the same with the second son, who had put the money in a business and had made a profit. The third son had hidden the money away and when his father asked him what he had done with it, he ran to recover it. When he showed the money to his father, it was taken away and that son was left with nothing.

The only way to be centered in self is to engage. Engagement lies in the choice to bring all parts of our life under the central influence of the truth of our situation. Evolution is the organizing principle and the growth around which our life centers.

DEENVELOPMENT EXERCISES

1   Balance is not the same as being centered. When a conflict arises between work and life or family and responsibilities, don't try to balance them out and "divide" your time. Always return to the truth of the situation to find ways in which what you choose to do in all areas of your life will be an expression of that higher truth. It is an illusion from our dualistic thinking that there are always two conflicting sides that cannot be reconciled. Family, love, work, time with others—all find meaning within the bigger picture and not within themselves.

2   Don't allow one set of emotional or thinking patterns to overrun from one circumstance into another. This is the cause of most conflict and argument. Being busy can cause everything to be dealt with in the same "get it done" way, where personal pressures dictate at the expense of any real growth or effectiveness. Putting out fires is pointless if you are trying to increase the heat.

3   Don't be self-centered unless you tell yourself you are going to be so. You cannot just change from being self-centered to being centered in a higher truth or principle simply because you feel like it. It is a slowly developing process of change. At least by choosing to be self-centered and telling others to be patient for the next hour because you are going to be selfish about this issue has the effect of making it less important and is a mark of great leadership, since others will not confuse the self-centered you with the real higher-centered you.

DEVELOPMENT EXERCISES

1   Actively seek to be of service to a greater truth than just yourself. Integrity is its own reward. Don't shortcut the truth—you cannot win that way. Winning is a threefold principle that allows the self, the other person, and the principle all to grow. Have in mind that "losing" in your identity so that the principle can win is an act of high leadership and signals that engagement is "safe." Contrive to let your identity lose so that your core can win *in what is real*.

2   Approach each and every situation afresh by mentally cutting off from the last situation. This can be done with a simple three-part mental procedure: evaluate what has just happened, find some meaning in it, then leave it behind and start afresh.

3   Practice telling yourself what you are going to do and why and from what principle and then doing it. Running through it in your mind aligns you to the principle from which you choose to act. Don't use principles retroactively to explain what you have done; adopt principles (they are after all principles—first things) from which you can do what you choose. Even a simple act such as weeding the garden or clearing up your desk can serve the conscious development of the principle to separate what you don't want to grow from what you do want to grow. Choosing the principle first makes a simple behavior a powerful and focused act!

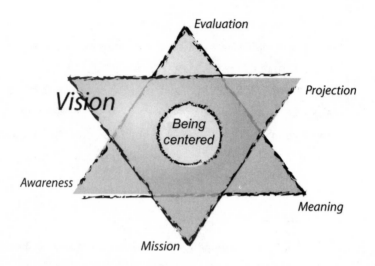

The next three steps form what I call the "triune of action." In the first three steps we were concerned to understand the truth of the situation and in Step Four we considered what it means to be centered in that truth. In the next three steps we are going to see how to act from the truth of the situation.

Walking the talk is very difficult when we are a divided self and quite natural when we are a unified self. When we seek only short-term results from a short-sighted vision of making things work or putting things right according to our view, we are prone to impose our dominance on events. We will look at how to take the blinkers off our self-conditioning and do far more than even we may believe we are capable of.

Seeing afresh is the great warrior stance of the SQ individual, beginning each day and each moment anew and taking nothing for granted. Vision is not based in seeing some grand scheme with ourselves at the center of the action, it is seeing that even in the smallest things the event of living meaningfully is possible.

9

Step Five: Vision

The real voyage of discovery consists not in finding new lands but in seeing with new eyes.

Marcel Proust

In Tibetan Buddhism the notion of mind is structured into the temporary, changing mind and the permanent, unchanging mind. Sogyal Rinpoche wonderfully demonstrates this in his book *The Tibetan Book of Living and Dying*.

The first is the ordinary mind, called by the Tibetans Sem. Sem is the discursive, dualistic mind which can only function in relation to a projected and falsely perceived external reference point. That which possesses discriminating awareness, that which possesses a sense of duality—which grasps or rejects something external—that is Sem.

Then there is the nature of mind; its innermost essence, which is absolutely and always untouched by change or death. At present it is hidden within our mind, our Sem, enveloped and obscured by the mental scurry of our thoughts and emotions ... In Tibet we call it Rigpa, a primordial, pure pristine awareness that is at once

intelligent, cognisant, radiant and always awake. It could be said
to be the knowledge of knowledge itself.

Rinpoche also describes the shift from seeking permanent truth
(the changes laid out in Steps One, Two, and Three) to actually
occupying the permanent truth of our self:

In Tibetan Buddhism there is a shock practice used to precisely
cause this result ...
When the young Sogyal was alone with his master, the master
said, "Now I am going to introduce you to the essential nature of
mind." Picking up his bell and small hand drum, he chanted the
invocation to the masters of the lineage, from the primordial
Buddha down to his own master. Then he did the introduction.
Suddenly he sprang on me a question with no answer, "What is
mind?" and gazed intently deep into my eyes. I was taken totally
by surprise. My mind shattered. No words, no names, no thoughts
remained—no mind, in fact at all.
Past thoughts had died away, the future had not yet arisen; the
stream of my thoughts was cut right through. In that shock a pure
gap opened, and in that gap was laid bare a sheer immediate
awareness of the present ... and that naked simplicity was also
radiant with the warmth of an immense compassion.

Some years ago, I was locked in a deep dialog with the man to
whom this book is dedicated, Leo Armin. In all my life I had not
met such an individual. I felt an implicit and explicit trust born
not just from my intuition but from years of education at his
hands. There was no subject on which his intelligence did not
cast some new light.

Leo had been describing to me that inside each of us there
is a deeper state, something locked that seeks liberation and ful-

fillment that is very potent but not readily seen or accessed. It is not easy to get to, he said. Until we are able to access that inner core, we are bound to repeat the same experiences again and again. "In you," he said, "this inner core is particularly powerful and you will never settle until you find a way to release it."

The engagement between us was so intense that I had no awareness of anything other than that I was looking into the eyes of someone I trusted deeply, the only man from whom I did not need to hide. I hadn't noticed that he was holding a mirror at the level of his waist, outside of my field of vision. At some point he said, "I want to give you an experience to help you release that very powerful state that is within you." Slowly he spoke about this inner state and as he said the words "and the truth of this state is right here," he placed the mirror in front of him so my own eyes were suddenly reflected back at me. I was staring at myself as if for the first time.

I was completely taken aback. I had not had the chance to prepare myself with my usual preconditioned response. No doubt if I had seen the mirror before I would have thought, "I wonder what is going on, is he going to put the mirror in front of me? What will that be like?" I would probably have contrived an expression as we do when walking along a street anticipating a shop window in which we know we will look at ourselves.

In the unanticipated moment I had no fear, no kind of negative emotion, but was thrown into a new sense of self. I felt compassion for every living thing in that moment and an incalculable time afterward. I saw all things differently from a different mind. I had no desire to compete or win over others, but only that each and every person should find the best of themselves and succeed.

Looking back on this moment, I can attribute all kinds of meanings to what happened. I could say that a great teacher was helping to release me from my dependence and by causing me to look inside myself was putting me in the driving seat. Or I could say that the distinction between other things and myself was broken and I experienced a sense of the interconnectedness of all things. But it wouldn't be true. The state was one that I had never known before in that way. It was not mediated through other experiences that I had already known.

I was uniquely aware that my eyes were soft and carried an energy that passed to others for several days and all the dealings I had with people were eased and assisted. Beyond my everyday reality there was another state, powerful and intense, full of knowledge and wisdom and yet little understood. I believe this experience helped me immeasurably to locate a stillness and deeper core from that time onward, from which I began to see what I had never been able to see. I believe that only a person of the highest wisdom could have passed this experience on to me.

Seeing with new eyes

Step Five challenges the general assumption that action is a combination of sweat and exertion. The man of action, forever on the move, putting out fires, solving problems, being involved in everyone's business, firing off commands, delegating actions to be taken—this could not be further from what real and effective action is.

The SQ basis of action begins with seeing what can be done. This is only possible once we understand the truth of the situation and are centered in its principles.

Below are some examples of principles that are at the core of real action. In each case, they integrate the division mentality that prevents correct evaluation, by developing a singular but higher level of vision. Each of these principles expresses the permanent truth we witness in the ways nature conducts its affairs: the freshness of a brand new day, the order of the seasons, the patterns of growth, the chains of interdependence of all living things.

❖ Affirming life.
❖ Never leaving a situation less than you find it.
❖ Keeping things clean and tidy as a daily routine.
❖ Generating the intelligence with which others may succeed.
❖ Starting each day and each situation afresh.
❖ Leaving each day clearly and cleanly.
❖ Always working for good results for all.
❖ Being upfront in expressing your reasons and intentions rather than concealing them to gain advantage.

Take just one example, never leaving a situation less than you find it, and consider how much this one principle would change the way we act in every situation. It would mean we would make an uncommon effort with everyone we deal with and in every situation. It would encourage us to employ the arts and skills and bring quality to every process. We couldn't idly dismiss others and blame them for what goes wrong, overriding them, ignoring their feelings and their contribution. We couldn't leave a situation messy, unresolved, and full of conflict.

Acting from this principle is truly visionary and can be applied every day, every moment. It is above all an expression of the adult intelligence that understands that an attitude of continually taking and never contributing is contrary to the laws of life.

Vision is a choice to see what really *is*. By connecting to spiritual intelligence at our core, we cannot *not* see. Seeing or vision is a function of developing consciousness.

I have been in many situations where a company or a group of people asked me how to develop a vision of the future. My answer is always in the same area, though hopefully fresh each time. To paraphrase Proust, "Vision is seeing with new eyes not seeing new lands."

We have discussed the principle that what we see is largely conditioned by what we have already seen. The versions of the "future" we fashion are largely based on the "past" that we have experienced. SQ, as ever, looks for the missing third system, not straining our eyes to see further than what we already expect to find, but looking with new eyes to see what is often right in front of our eyes but we may not normally see.

A school that I visited with my wife last year had grasped this principle exactly. At the end of the final lesson of the day, the children, aged 8 and 9, began to clean up their own area. They brushed their space clean with brooms, just as the teacher did. We asked why they did this.

"All the children and the teacher need to approach the day afresh. This is our daily practice to ensure that when we arrive tomorrow it is truly a fresh start."

It is a wise person who chooses to keep their inner and outer space clean and clear. Yesterday's unresolved problems can easily become the trigger for tomorrow's reactions.

As teachers seeks to be fresh and new each day, they are naturally more engaging to the children. Children know the difference between regurgitated knowledge and new discoveries— just as we know fresh food from pre-packaged food. Teachers who are excluded from their own core by an identity that assumes it is better than the children and doesn't need to be alive and engaging, who expects to be listened to, followed, and respected, can only evaluate the children from their own IQ and EQ identity of self. This is the same in all walks of life.

The event horizon

From our materially based, emotionally attached selves, we may look into the future and find that our vision is cut off by what science calls an event horizon (Figure 11). We often say that we can't see what to do when we face a problem.

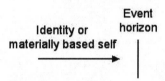

Figure 11 The event horizon

Our SQ self extends far beyond that horizon where our physical sight has a cutoff point (Figure 12).

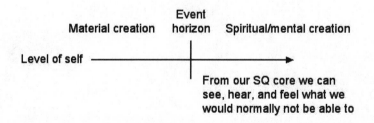

Figure 12 Seeing beyond the event horizon

The story of human evolution tells how we have gone beyond that event horizon time and time again. Events that we consider ultimate are continually being surpassed, influenced by a higher level of intelligence.

In this book we have referred to many individuals who have seemed to be working simultaneously toward the development of SQ. Sometimes they were even working on the same developments at the same time on different sides of the world, clearly tuning in to the same higher intelligence. Charles Darwin, author of *The Origin of Species*, illustrates just such a synchronicity. In *The Ascent of Man*, Bronowski explains:

> *When Darwin did hit on an explanation for the evolution of species two years later, he was reluctant to publish it. He might have put it off all his life, if a very different kind of man had not also followed almost exactly the same steps of experience and thought that moved Darwin, and arrived at the same theory. His name was Alfred Russel Wallace.*

It is fascinating how trends in knowledge or music or art or thought can sweep across the world as a wave of new intelligence. Even the fact that Beethoven and Mozart met for an hour (Mozart coming to Beethoven's house for composition class and being called away because his father was suddenly taken ill) seems strangely meaningful. I am yet to read a convincing explanation of this phenomenon, but dismissing it as mere "coincidence" fails to explain anything.

The human face—a window for intelligence

Vision is more than seeing. It suggests an energy that can awaken a faculty of the brain and mind that can see beyond the event horizon, beyond the known. This energy is the SQ intelligence that is observable in both the face of the SQ individual and the light of joy in the eyes of children.

Paul Eckman, world-renowned psychologist and expert on the human face, recently spent a week in India with the Dalai Lama in conference with other scientists and some of the top Lamas of Tibet. The subject of their forum was the emotions and specifically how to develop constructive emotions. An account of the week is written up in a book called *Destructive Emotions* by Daniel Goleman.

While accustomed to making scientific appraisals based on measurable features in the brain using the latest and most up-to-date scanning equipment, Eckman's observations on what qualities he found in the Dalai Lama are highly significant. Not one of the characteristics he notes can be scientifically measured. The four qualities that distinguish the spiritual individual, according to Eckman, are:

❖ A palpable goodness.
❖ An impression of selflessness, a lack of concern with status, fame, and ego. A transparency between their personal and public lives.
❖ Compassionate energy that nourishes others.
❖ Amazing powers of attentiveness.

Goleman relates a conversation Eckman had with the Dalai Lama:

As his daughter, Eve, asked the Dalai Lama a personal question about relationships, His Holiness alternately held and affectionately rubbed each of their hands. That small encounter, Paul later recounted, was what some people would call a mystical transforming experience. "I was inexplicably suffused with physical warmth during those five to ten minutes—a wonderful kind of warmth throughout my body and face. It was palpable. I felt a kind of goodness I'd never before felt in my life all the time I sat there."

A similar flow of energy is experienced by people in many walks of life, from actors to musicians to sports people. As intense as this experience can be, it describes how a permanent truth and the permanent self together create a flow of intelligence, the greater SQ and the SQ core of self. The body and brain seem to (and actually do) slow down and there is little or no difference between what we do and the inner principle of self that is doing —there is a level of integration, of active congruence where we are walking our talk.

What is remarkable about those we call spiritually intelligent is the permanence of this state. The Dalai Lama, Gandhi, the later pictures of Nelson Mandela all have an energy in their eyes.

Interestingly enough, Eckman confirms the point I make throughout this book: "It wasn't luck or culture or genes that created this qualitative difference. These people have resculpted their brains through practice." Neuroscience would add that contrary to the prevailing theories until the late 1980s our brains can be resculpted and are not hardwired. We are not in the grip of nurture and nature only—we are able by choice to superimpose a new experience on the brain, if we can find that experience, and that requires a new level of intelligence.

There are three clearly distinct and separate areas of the face operated by three different nerves from the trigeminal nerves.

The lower part of the face is most clearly the area where we ruminate about matters—we talk about "chewing things

IQ, EQ, and SQ—Visible in the face

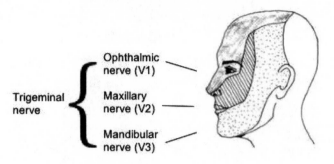

over," "making a meal of it," trying to "digest" some matter or another. This area of the face expresses those IQ levels, generally speaking, that are more at the material end of our IQ chain of being.

The middle part of the face corresponds to what we have been calling EQ. It includes the nose area, which significantly is connected to what was once called the nose brain, the rhinencephalon. This is the limbic area in the mid brain that includes the hippocampus and amygdala (so important to our emotional responses). The most ancient root of our emotional life is our sense of smell, the olfactory lobe that functions in the analysis of the content of smell. All life carries a distinctive smell that is its molecular signature and since it can be transferred in the wind, it enables the detection of that which is familiar and that which is not, that which may be a threat and that which is known and friendly. This was once a vital feature of our daily survival. We talk about "having a nose for things," "smelling a good idea," "sniffing out" the truth, as if an idea or a truth, similarly, has a molecular structure that we can analyse and detect.

The most notable mark of emotional engagement lies in a smile and the most noticeable mark of emotional disengagement lies in when the muscles of this middle area of the face are flattened rather than animated. It is interesting to note that to produce a real smile—a Duchene smile as it is termed after its discoverer Guillaume Duchene—rather than a fake smile requires a genuine reason to smile, a "why to" to know "how to." We can voluntarily activate many of the muscles that make a real smile but some, notably those that crinkle the muscles around the eyes and turn up the corners of the mouth, are not accessed voluntarily.

The third area, which significantly includes the eyes, is the part of our face where, as Eckman notes, the light of our inner intelligence can shine out with "a compassionate energy that nourishes others." The eyes, quite literally extensions of the brain, can carry a person's active inner SQ intelligence. Audrey Hepburn once made the observation that to have beautiful eyes one must look to see the good in others.

Perhaps nowhere was this made clearer to me than when I saw a picture of the American author Helen Keller. She was not only deaf and dumb but blind from the age of nineteen months and yet her eyes shone with a remarkable kindness and understanding that were quite radiant.

This is quite contrary to the way my doctor looks out of the window when I tell him my symptoms. I have noticed this tendency in managers and leaders alike, and I know it is actually trained into psychologists as a means of depersonalizing the doctor–patient association. For a doctor to be emotionally involved in each patient would be exhausting and inappropriate—that is not what I am suggesting.

However, there is a way of SQ looking in which we can be engaged in a live event full of meaning and promise. When we look in this SQ way at another person, we are able to see the far-back causes of why they have come to be the way they are and this promotes vital understanding and compassion.

We talk about people "lighting up the room," "being bright," "shining examples," "illuminated," and so on. This suggests a further level of our evolution—the clear sight or vision that can see beyond the material realm. To see what others have not yet seen is of course a great evolutionary advantage, and is a sign of the visionary.

DEENVELOPMENT EXERCISES

1   Try not to look at things too hard or fixedly or get too involved in details. Become aware of the way stress causes you to see less and less about the depths of the person or thing you are looking at, which impairs your evaluation faculties.

2   Looking is very much influenced by posture and mental state and the way you look is habitual and mostly limits what you can see. As an example, before you look at someone you have had difficulty dealing with, stand with your feet slightly apart and your head pushed a little back (not with your jaw jutting forward) and look as if you are gazing broadly at a landscape of which they are a part. Don't make them the center of the world, but see that they are part of it.

3   Give up the idea that you can't see what to do, that you can't "see your way through" any particular situation. You cannot afford to just be a passenger and sit on the sidelines. Don't divide life into times when you act and times when you relax. Even sitting in a doctor's waiting room is an opportunity to act constructively, if you can see the truth of the situation. Become an intelligence finder who sees new intelligence opportunities for challenges that the world faces—they are never yours alone if they are real challenges. Send messages, write, communicate your new intelligence insights to others, even if the challenge they face is not yours personally. Train yourself to see new solutions in all aspects of life and not merely those that become overbearing problems.

DEVELOPMENT EXERCISES

1 There are many ways to respect who and what we are looking at. "Re-spect" literally means to look again and it carries
with it the quality of looking with new eyes. If you find yourself
judging others from an out-of-centered self, remind yourself
that what you are looking at is new, first time, not known.
Simply look away for a moment and try to see afresh.

2 Try to look at people with the mental idea that they are a
potential field of intelligence and for all kinds of reasons may
have become stuck and excluded from the potential that they
are. Try to look afresh and feel the far-back reasons that may
have caused them to be stuck where they are. You will see a
different face, different stresses, different tensions and pains
that overlay the inner face, which was formed by their childhood nature that longs to grow but is imprisoned. Once you
really see, you can really *do*.

3 In each situation see something to do that improves the intelligence that is present, even if this means clearing up the
room or office to create better harmonies that allow clearer
thinking. Leadership doesn't worry about being seen to be
demeaning—its protection is its reasons and principles. Practice acting from the principle and not from the need to act on
the problem directly. See ways to work around issues to allow
new opportunities to be seen—you don't have to be the one
who always solves everything. If nothing else, spread good
humor, practice storytelling, being interesting, search and
explore, clean the space and ready it for things to happen—
there is so much to do when you really see.

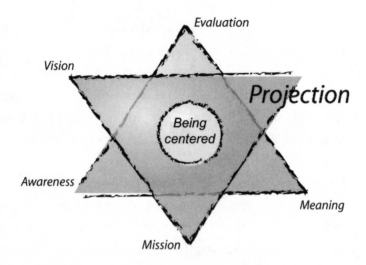

In this step we are going to look at the way we project toward the future. Steps Five and Six work together, hand in hand.

When we see what can be done from the truth of the situation, we project the intelligence with which to do it. No matter how visionary the idea, it is the level of intelligence we project that will govern what is able to happen.

Real self-leadership is the way of SQ projection. Rather than trying to find great acts and deeds to attempt to convince ourselves and others that we are making a difference, SQ projects new intelligence into the world that others can benefit from.

10

Step Six: Projection

In the film *Field of Dreams*, Kevin Costner plays an Iowa farmer called Ray Kinsella. With his wife and daughter, Ray works the cotton fields trying to make a living off their small farm. In time and with a few bad harvests, he faces the inevitable. Even family and friends believe it is their duty to convince him that the farm needs to be closed down and sold. It is never going to turn a profit. They have his best interests at heart, they say. But Ray has a dream he is holding on to. He has been out at night in the cornfields and heard a voice whispering to him: "Build it and he will come."

When he confides in his wife she is none too convinced. "Build what and who will come?" she asks in disbelief.

As the film unfolds, Ray discovers that some of the greats of baseball who have died are urging him to build a baseball diamond so they can return and play again. Ray's belief in the project, against all odds, not only breathes new life into him but his bank account too.

It's an enthralling story that makes a distinction between projecting to a known future and an unknown future. The insight of the film is that when we are committed utterly to something, even if it seems impossible, it can happen. The projection needs to leave space for what we want to happen that we are not always able to predict. In fact this occurs regularly in everyday life but we may not consciously be aware of it.

In our everyday use of the term projection, we might envisage ourselves casting our mind forward to some known target, as an archer might take aim with an arrow in his bow. Projection precedes action. Projection calculates the trajectory to some clear target where success is the bull's eye of a direct hit and each segment away from that small targeted area defines the inaccuracy of the projection. Companies, governments, and individuals have targets, be it higher sales figures, lower crime figures, or being able to afford to go away on holiday. To check our projections we ask: "Are we on target?"

The SQ individual aims not at a material goal, to increase it in terms of more profits, a bigger income, or longer or more exotic holidays. After all, we are always saying that material things alone don't make for success or happiness. The SQ projection is always to bring new levels of intelligence to the situation to cause two things:

❖ a decrease in ignorance (identity) and those conditions that promote ignorance;

❖ an increased conscious projection of new conditions in which new ideas and new intelligence are able to flourish.

The SQ individual is not projecting to known results but projecting from new intelligence, an intelligence that doesn't alter the outcomes but changes what is possible. This requires the conscious application of self, and not just a reactive level of self. To predict what will happen is to understand not simply the laws of cause and effect (the two-intelligence model) but the projection of a new space, in which a new intelligence process can take root that will bring about new results. This is the three-intelligence model.

Listen to what New York mayor Rudolf Guiliani says in his book *Leadership*, describing what has come to be known as the "broken windows theory":

> *The theory holds that a seemingly minor matter like broken windows in abandoned buildings leads directly to a more serious degeneration of neighborhoods. Someone who wouldn't normally throw a rock at an intact building is less reluctant to break a second window in a building that already has one broken. And someone emboldened by all the second broken windows may do even worse damage if he senses that no one is around to prevent lawlessness.*

Broken windows are not the worst of New York's problems, but in mending them something more is being addressed than just their repair. It is the environment of not caring, apathy, lowering accepted standards, and lack of will. Just as the attitude "why not?" declares an empty, meaningless intelligence, the question "why?" heralds the opportunity for a new intelligence.

This is a fine example of how in SQ the projection is not at a target but from a level of self that has explored why things happen the way they do. It is the insistence on standards, good order, care, and neighborhood pride that brings change.

SQ projection leaves space for other sequences, other events to be initiated than those we project. SQ projection is an invitation to new levels and new intelligence. To project only to targets is only to succeed in what is known.

SQ is not goal driven. The goals that we target are usually material results that can be measured in figures that seem compelling to the IQ and EQ intelligences. Crime is down, sales are up. The difficulty we have in projecting at targets is that life is not one thing, or many "one things," all on a material plane. Of course, no one can deny that a city with less crime is desirable, as are better public services, more hospital beds, and so on, but happiness and a greater purpose in life are not measurable by plotting figures in the same way.

Individual happiness is also not greatly enhanced by reaching targets that are materially based. There is increasingly a view in positive psychology that each of us has a "happiness level," an emotional "given" that is little increased or decreased by material gains or rewards—and yet we aim ourselves at these same targets again and again.

Projection needs to begin in the settlement of self, in Step Four, and in the vision of the great wealth that can be achieved when one truly sees the truth of the situation (Step Five). Projection is not aiming at a result that our identity has been convinced of as being worthy, it is aiming from a level of self that sustains new initiatives in the world.

Projecting from imbalance

One of the difficulties with projecting ourselves toward a target is that we never quite know where the projected action will end up. We are mostly shooting in the dark. We don't see (Step Five) where the projection stems from in ourselves until the result is clear and when we see the result we often need to make course corrections and refocus on another target.

What we sometimes call projection can be nothing more than expending energy to cover up the anxiety of being away from the core of ourselves. We project ourselves away from discomfort and anxiety in the hope that something will happen that makes a difference. Without being centered in self, we make projections too readily and we act based on too many assumptions, almost always with unfortunate results.

Projection from imbalance includes situations like the following:

❖ A parent sees their children behaving badly and wants to do something about it from the projection of what well-behaved kids would look like.

❖ A boss looks at the end-of-year reports and wants to set new projections for the following year that are signified by a rise in profits.

❖ A country feels threatened by another nation and wants to make sure it is stopped, so it projects an accord.

We see something wrong and we want to put it "right." This is a dualistic process.

A divided self assumes that what it consigns as wrong it can put right. Our projections are aimed at causing results that alter the issue we think needs fixing. We want the children to behave better, we want there to be increased sales in the next quarter, we want the country in question to stop being a threat. Let's call this target point of desired result point B.

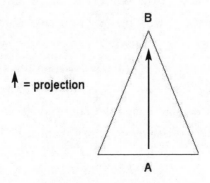

Our projection is aimed from point A, what we identify as "wrong," to point B, where we want things to end up. Take the example of children behaving badly. We take the kids to task, believing this will "sort out" the problem, but soon a new issue comes up. The children "behave" better but are resentful and less engaged because they have been told off. We now redefine the issue that needs to be sorted out as being the fact that they are acting resentfully, at point C and no longer at point B. So we make another projection about point C to sort out their resentfulness and lack of engagement. We give the children a treat to make them more energized, happier, and less resentful.

B   **C**

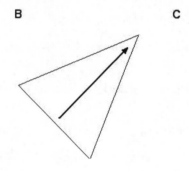

Point C is in a different direction from point B and now the kids are confused, since our line of projection doesn't seem consistent. They may be appeased by the treat but have discovered that they can behave badly and if the parents threaten punishment they can act sullen and still profit by getting treats. They have learnt how to manipulate their parents into giving them what they want, so they play on this and develop shifting behaviors by pulling emotional strings, which builds poor character. The parents become unpredictable and the children never know which of their portrayals to trust, (angry, compliant, guilty, forgiving, and so on).

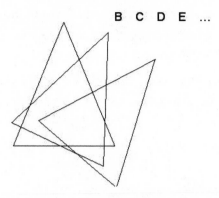

The lesson: Be sure of the inner principle that you project from! Look back at point A. It is not the children's behavior that is the awareness one should be reacting to but *why* they are behaving badly.

SQ projection is not aimed at such specific end results and doesn't keep reacting from ever more minute details in the apex of the triune, but is committed action from a broad-based principle of higher truth that it believes in time will bring about a more appropriate result. The projection of self that comes from the bigger picture is not aimed at the end result but at establishing and expanding the domain of higher truth, where the right things can flourish and the wrong things cannot.

The viewpoint of the seven steps

Let's take the same example and look at it through the seven steps.

The children are misbehaving. If our awareness is too fight and flight based we are likely to react in Step Two to correct their behavior from the judgment in Step Three that they are "wrong" by acting the way they do. This centers us in being "right" and causes division between us and the children. From this division all kinds of resentment, antagonism, and conflict will arise in time. We simply are not understanding the situation in anything other than identity terms—our experience and our version of the truth versus theirs. This will lead to imbalanced actions to "correct" their faults without ever looking inside ourselves to find a new intelligence that enables self and the children to rejoin each other in a new harmony.

Let's restart the process. The SQ individual is aware that the children are behaving in a certain way, the meaning of which they see will lead to unfortunate consequences in the short or long term. The parent's evaluation of this is that the children are missing some part of their education or knowledge or ability to handle the experience in a centered way. It may be any number of factors that the parent detects: the children may be modeling their behavior on a television program or someone at school, they may be rebelling because they didn't feel listened to at breakfast that morning, and so on. Somehow the natural SQ/EQ/IQ harmonies in the children have been disrupted and need to be restored.

The centered and engaged parent will come to *see* the situation clearly, but they must give it time and not think that quick action will rectify the imbalance. Let's say the parent sees that the children are simply not confident enough to make their own choices and are resorting to copying others.

Here SQ vision will help lift the parent from being a reactive or corrective force to being a self-leader and a leader to their children. They will see that the skills and intelligence to make their own choices need to be provided or strengthened in the children and this is a task they project to do. It may be accomplished by talks, demonstrations, insights, and questions, but it will not be enforced by threat and punishment.

So, the actions that Steps Five and Six undertake are consistent with and congruent with the understanding of the situation. Vision and projection will deliver new levels of intelligence and conscious action and create a safe field of intelligence for personal and collective growth in any number of areas:

❖ seeing how to initiate projects that provide greater security for the children in making mistakes;

❖ providing space for a dialog about how to act, how to be, and why;

❖ spending time with the children to educate them in how powerful choice is, how to make good choices, how to understand the truth of each and every situation;

❖ giving some more room to expend the tensions that naturally build up in children in the teenage years when so many new things are faced.

The same principles apply to any human interaction. Aiming merely at known targets gets short-term results; aiming at growth and increasing intelligence develops long-term satisfaction in all kinds of ways.

Project it and it will happen

Last Sunday a pleasant family—mother, father, and two girls—knocked at our door. The woman was holding out a box and asked if I would like to donate to the Red Cross. It wasn't an invasive act, they were courteous and well mannered. I felt inclined to give them some money and was on the point of getting my wallet when I realized that it was in fact the pressure of the situation I was reacting to, not the charitable cause. I could have argued the point with myself and thought "I'll just put some money in the box," but this would have had no meaning.

"I wonder if you could tell me the direction you are going next?" I asked. "It's just that I don't know what I think about this and would like to take a few minutes to work it out." They looked at me quizzically, as if they had heard some excuses in their time but this one really took the prize. Nevertheless, they pointed to some houses in the next street where they were going and off they went, I suspect fairly sure they would never set eyes on me again.

When I considered it, what I did see was the principles they were committed to and clearly demonstrating: their willingness to do what is good and helpful and to actively contribute to a better state of affairs. About 10 minutes later, I set off along the street and found the family again. With the same courteous manner they were asking another couple if they would like to donate.

"Excuse me," I said, catching their attention. They looked amazed to see me. "I gave it some thought and while I don't know yet whether I intend to support this particular charity, I do want to support the principle of what you are doing. Your willingness to give your time and effort to support a good cause is really remarkable." I put some money in the box and thanked them. I knew why I was donating the money—the material result may look the same but the intelligence was very different.

Some weeks later they passed our house again. The mother remarked, "You know, sometimes it is quite hard to go round with a box and have people think that all you are doing is collecting money. But what you said made us want to keep going. You really seemed to understand why we are doing this and that is worth more than any amount of money."

Goethe makes the point eloquently:

Until one is committed, there is the hesitancy, the chance to draw back, always ineffectiveness, concerning all acts of initiative (and creation). There is one elementary truth the ignorance of which kills countless ideas and splendid plans: that the moment one definitely commits oneself then providence moves too. All sorts of things occur to help one that would never otherwise have occurred ... Whatever you can do or dream you can, begin it. Boldness has genius, power, and magic in it. Begin it now!

I believe that we are often closer to these ways of acting than we give ourselves credit for. Perhaps it is because our dualistic model of mind and matter fails to provide a way of interpreting events that are essentially SQ. We often project our action into the unknown, believing that something will happen. We call it hope when it fails and belief when it succeeds. Commitment is the difference.

Walt Disney was looking for a site for a park that he had seen in his mind's eye. One day he was standing in a field with some real estate agents and some advisers. Was this the right place, what would be the costs, the practicalities, tax considerations, building permissions, and so on? Disney was standing quietly to the side.

One of the group drew one last time on his cigarette and threw the stub down, grinding it into the earth. Disney bent down and picked it out of the earth. "Would you kindly not put out your cigarette in the entrance area to the park?" he gently chided the man. Some months later, at this precise spot, stood the gates to the park entrance.

It is not enough to want good in this world—SQ believes it is possible too.

DEENVELOPMENT EXERCISES

1   When you see something about another person that you dis-
like or feel inclined to blame, don't fix on it in the other person
and fill it with power that can only serve to amplify it in them
(and you). Doing this merely trains your mind to fix the level
of the intelligence available in any given situation and this
prevents you finding new solutions from new levels.

2   Never project problems that you think are going to occur or
load situations toward a nonproductive outcome. This uses
your very subtle and advanced communication systems to
project cues to let others know that the intelligence you are
projecting will not allow anything other than a "negative" outcome. Always work to overcome the identity in yourself that
would have you believe that a situation is "impossible."

3   Stop projecting ill-defined and assumptive portrayals of self
such as "I want to make a difference," "I want to do something
great while I am alive," and the emotional pressures that
accompany these. The pressure to be seen to be or feel yourself doing something important will distract from the ability to
recognize that being alive is itself the projection of a huge
importance.

DEVELOPMENT EXERCISES

1   Take on the problems of the world and try to solve them in yourself so that you will be able to lead others to find their own solutions. If another person's lack of understanding makes them brittle and difficult to deal with, to help them is to reawaken your own intelligence about the wisest ways you have found to deal with this challenge—in yourself.

2   Project the values and principles that you want to serve and learn to suffer the history of experiences that might suggest nothing can be done. Choose to suffer for the sake of the principle and suffer it gladly—but that doesn't mean suffer fools gladly. Suffer the struggle for new intelligence to appear and evolve against the opposition of history.

3   Projection of self is not to a known result, it is to the increase of intelligence than enables new levels of outcome. Project clear wisdom through yourself about challenges that the world is dealing with ignorantly and in time you will find yourself included more and more in actively serving those challenges. Practice projecting impossible outcomes—that war will stop, for example. It will accustom your projection powers to much larger fields of influence than whether you get a parking ticket or not. This is the story of all great people: they didn't wait to be great, they were great while they waited for the opportunity to serve greatness.

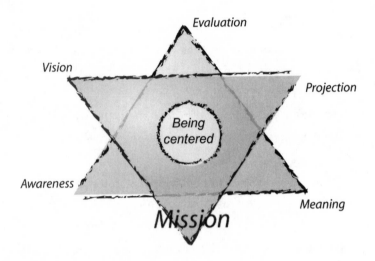

In the last of the seven steps we will be able to distinguish between a disconnected sense of mission and a real SQ sense of mission.

We shall see that an SQ sense of mission is not something we work out and say we are going to pursue. It is unifying our self with the truth of the situation. It is becoming conscious and recognizing that our unique contribution in living in the world is in being able to express the truth of the situation directly. Mission is not "trying" to be an example, it is walking our talk.

Our sense of mission has been developed through the previous six steps: awareness, meaning, evaluation, being centered, vision, and projection. The SQ sense of mission lies in knowing that what we do is exactly an expression of why we are here.

11

Step Seven: Mission

What I hear, I forget. What I see, I remember. What I do,
I understand.

Confucius

The first time I can recall hearing the word mission spoken with any significance was at school one Monday morning. The headmaster was addressing the whole assembly on the merits of a good education and to this end he brought our attention to the symbol and words emblazoned on our school jackets, "Rather death than false of faith." His speech reached a crescendo with the words, "Our mission is to be faithful to the goals of higher education."

I had only a very dim idea of what he might have been exalting (perhaps he was no clearer himself), but the moment was like a call to arms that quickened some inner pulse. To my young mind the motto and symbol of an eagle, claws raised, suggested that education was a serious business and that I was going to have to claw my way to success.

As we know, the mission statement has become an integral part of corporate identity and it too is meant to inspire those who rally to the banner. The mission statement might include what a company stands for, its values and its visions. It is analogous to the shields carried by the knights of the Middle Ages who wrote their mission statements in symbols and signs that were the projected self that the enemy would encounter if they dared to challenge them.

Of course, it is important to declare ourselves and be accountable to some level of truth. Our character or that of a relationship or a company is sustained and fortified by the truths it upholds.

There are two kinds of mission statement that I have come to distinguish over the years and each serves a very different but complementary purpose. The first is the kind of mission that acts as a beacon of sanity as we move through the middle, adolescent phase of our intelligence life (Figure 2), searching and exploring our self within a very varied world of experience. Just as in my school, such statements of mission provide us with a shield under which to work and explore the future in a safe and responsible way.

Reviewing some of the sessions I have conducted over the years with individuals and organizations, some of the most common themes of this first kind of mission statement have been:

❖ To provide first-class service to our customers.
❖ To be the best in our field.
❖ To champion excellence in our industry.
❖ To create a harmonious team where every person is respected for their contribution.
❖ To make a significant difference in the lives of others.
❖ To act with honesty and integrity.

As I said, these act as beacons to keep our minds focused in the right direction and are based in semipermanent truths. However, no one would expect that just writing the words in a statement that is circulated in the office or having them engraved on a plaque and hanging that up in the entrance area will bring about any lasting change. People need to be more intimately bound up in the mission, feeling that by the character of what they do they contribute to its actualization. Let's call these "interim" missions.

Then there is a second kind of mission statement that is self-formed and "adult" (Figure 3) in the way it engages with unlimited potential. This kind of mission does not seek to actualize a material goal to "provide good service" or "increase productivity and profits." It recognizes a field of potential that can be seen ahead of and projected to, and its permanent truths embodied by and through personal or collective growth.

I can see no reason why a successful company or individual, who has acted with good character, fairness, and honesty and been guided by the first kind of mission, cannot rescript their mission statement to encompass a new core mission about what they are yet to become. The SQ mission, as we shall see, is a win–win–win situation for the individual, for others, and for the higher principle that allows us to win in new realms that we have yet to know or experience.

In this last step of the seven steps, I want to show how the SQ realms of mission are the conscious realization of our greater purpose and as such embody and integrate all the other steps.

The mechanics of mission

It has long been a contentious issue in brain science how the brain can function as a single entity. After all, the way we have mostly researched and explored the brain reflects the dichotomy that our dualistic model of intelligence encourages us to think with. On the one hand, we seem to be exploring the cavernous depths of an intricate mechanism where it is unclear how the many parts of the brain associate. On the other, we are exploring an entity that acts and behaves as if it is one unified whole. Which model of the brain is it most useful to adhere to? The answer, not surprisingly, is both.

Rodolfo Llinas, neuroscientist at New York University, poses the question with these words: "How are the separate bits of activity in different parts of the brain made into a single event?" Here we encounter our dualistic thinking in the language that characterizes the way the parts and the whole are made into a single event as a "how."

For a long time brain scientists searched inside the brain for signs of an inner homunculus that might explain how all the separate functions were controlled. However, even if they had found such a central intelligence it would hardly have solved the problem of who is controlling the brain. The question would continue in an infinite regress of asking who or what was the intelligence that controlled the brain of the homunculus. We have been fixed on finding how a singular control center might bring order to the many parts and this same pursuit characterizes the way we try to find organizing principles to control the many parts of our lives or the companies we run or are part of. We amalgamate, downsize, merge, centralize, or decentralize, but rarely discover the level of intelligence that allows natural integration.

We find it difficult to work within the idea that it is the integrating process itself, the "why," that brings unity to the divisions that we face. Please look at Figures 1, 2, and 3 again. They show the process by which what was once whole becomes divided, to become whole again at a new level. It is the promise of the great chain of our being to become rejoined and made whole again in adulthood—learning, feeling, and knowing, once more in harmony and unity.

The three-phase process is a description of the template of growth that we are able to see in diverse realms from cellular division right through to the evolution of the brain itself in becoming mindful, unified, and conscious.

Recognizing mission

The internal dialog we can hear in our brains expresses our sense of duality and the deep tensions of our state of division:

❖ I don't really know what to do with the rest of my life.

❖ Perhaps I should just take a break, get away from all this worry, live life for the moment.

❖ Why do I feel so unfulfilled and empty when I should be happy?

❖ Maybe I could go and have a drink, meet with some friends... But isn't that just avoiding the issue?

❖ How else can I find some peace and quiet?

Trying to still these inner voices with commands to be quiet or efforts to distract them into some other activity will never bring about any consensus or harmony among them. There is no central controller, as brain science now accepts, that can command order. This division is in fact the natural state of adolescence, and only by understanding why we are divided can we effectively become unified in engaging in a new phase of adult life. As I have tried to show throughout the book, it is by giving up the identity that thinks it can control how we function and by becoming a self that is engaged in new fields of intelligence that the contradictions become stilled. It is only by occupying the core of self that the level where no divisions exist can be occupied.

Mission brings the duality of self into a new relationship that serves a greater purpose.

Mission: a new script for a new time

We have all probably tried to script a mission statement at one time or another. We may begin by asking ourselves what we are going to accomplish with our life, emptying those ideas out on a sheet of paper, and starting to fashion them into a coherent statement that may then reflect back to us in the way of a criterion whether our actions conform or not. However, the point I have always made to companies and individuals who understand the need for a declaration of mission is that the process of scripting an SQ mission statement is not a mental act of conception. It is a mental elevation from which we are able to recognize that our lives have always been in partnership with the greatest criterion of all—the permanent truth of our situation. Just as I say in the section on the three levels of truth, a football game would be meaningless if there were no laws (semipermanent truth), so a life would be meaningless if there were no laws (permanent truth) that guide our self. Our part is to engage within the laws of the higher game.

The journey through the seven steps grows the consciousness of mission and the mission statement is an act of acknowledgment and recognition that through our life, the truth of the situation has always been the guiding influence to which we have in smaller or greater part been responsive. In childhood the truth of the situation caused our innermost core to be drawn to some field of intelligence or another, be it music or art, language or mathematics, sport or theater, acts of care or compassion. In adolescence we were caused to search and explore our self and in

adulthood the greater truth expresses itself in the conscious realization that there was always a higher intelligence guiding our life
through all three phases.

By being able to separate out those aspects of our life that
have been bound by identity and unrest from those aspects that
are rooted in a higher authority and meaning, we give wings to
the mission of our life. Every life has a mission and by conscious
recognition and review we are able to acknowledge it. Once
acknowledged, the self-value and inner settlement that it causes
are tangible and profound.

The mission statement in its most elevated form is the conscious declaration of self as a coherent part and partner of the
bigger picture—it is the reason we are here and the consciousness
of the meaningful part we have to play. The bigger picture is
expressed through all those who have been great. Greatness cannot be discovered just in what we do but in the release of new
intelligence that speaks or acts through us.

Take Mozart's music as an example. His name comes up
regularly when we talk of genius and we could acknowledge in a
general way that his mission in life was to make wonderful music,
but that doesn't clarify why his music is beyond the realms of being
good—it is great. In the last year or two we have discovered that
his music not only sounds beautiful but is synchronized with certain brain waves that actually cause an inner quiet and harmony
in the listener. Some hospitals in the UK have even begun playing
his *Eine Kleine Nachtmusik* to newborn infants and found that it
successfully calms and settles their anxieties in the weeks after
birth. As we are beginning to realize, Mozart's music is not only
emotionally satisfying, it is also functional in bringing a unifying
intelligence that settles and calms and quietens in those who know
how to listen. All great music, theater, art, and speech has this
effect of allowing us to listen to the deep core of our self becoming.

Anyone who is familiar with Marianne Williamson's writing will be able to follow the exact sequence of the seven steps as her words unfold. It is the intelligence her words releases that has the overwhelming impact. It is the difference between something good and something great. In *A Return to Love* she says:

> *Our deepest fear is not that we are inadequate. Our deepest fear is that we are powerful beyond measure ... We were born to make manifest the glory of God that is within us. It is not just in some of us; it is in everyone. And as we let our own light shine, we unconsciously give other people permission to do the same. As we are liberated from our own fear, our presence automatically liberates others.*

The recognition of our SQ mission is only possible by and through the elevation of self to a new level through the seven steps and this is accomplished by allowing the more illumined core to shine out. SQ mission is the ultimate self-leadership—it "automatically liberates others."

A personal story

Among the many rich and varied insights I have had during my years of training, one thing became abundantly clear to me and has influenced all my dealings with other people: no one can make this journey of development for another person.

The inner trigger to change involves timing and alignment, knowledge and many other subtle factors. I was infinitely fortunate that the groundwork for understanding was indelibly engraved in me through the years, so when the opportunity to change did present itself I was able to seize the moment. This is in fact the importance of the seven steps: they provide a template by which to view our life experience and opportunity as it happens.

Some years ago my life came to the most abrupt halt. Within a short period both my mother and father died, my work ended, I lost all my money on a well-intentioned but stupid venture, and my health declined considerably. I have always prided myself on being able to pick myself up and start again and could have done so on this occasion—but I didn't. I sat for two days and tried to figure out what to do, what was the wise course of action, where to go next, why I found myself in this crisis at this point in my life.

As I sat there, my thoughts and emotions span round in an orbit that I knew so well. There was the internal resolve not to be deflated, the edge of not allowing myself to become depressed or sink, the overwhelming feeling that this must have some meaning but being too self-reflective simply to live on maxims like "life teaches us the lessons we need" or "God tests those he loves the most." I found no solace in being one of God's chosen experiments at that moment—it was far too simplistic an explanation.

Toward the end of the second day I hatched a plan that made financial, even emotional sense, but there was a very substantial inner sense that something fundamental was missing. I saw that all I was considering was orbiting about me, my realms of understanding within my limited experience. I saw through myself in a way that allowed me to understand the man in the Netherlands whose story I told earlier who felt so empty. I realized that even my emotional gloom was more about the fact that this was appropriate emotional behavior as I had learnt it and not real. If I had but realized it, I was in fact starting a new phase of my life.

Our house overlooked a lake and the terrace from my office had a splendid view across the water. I went outside on the terrace, but rather than I doing what I always did and gazing across this lovely scene, I turned round and looked into the room in which I had spent so many years working. In those moments I came to understand the person that was used to being in there. I become a kind of observer of my own life. I saw the computer, the pictures of my parents, my wife, the books I had collected, the layout of the room—and I found myself wondering why I had arranged my life like this. I saw myself as if for the first time. I saw that my identity could easily spend the rest of its life writing and lecturing and continuing in pretty much the same way—and I know that in that moment I chose not to. Something had come into my awareness and I was trying to understand my life from a bigger picture.

I saw a photograph on my desk of myself as a young boy and recalled how in those early years I had been deeply affected by others in pain and had so wanted to respond in this awareness but found little wisdom for action. Where had this knowing gone? From my life experience and search for truth I knew intellectually that the greatest suffering any person can experience is the ignorance of why we are here. Suddenly in that moment I knew it again with all of my intelligences. It was not just an intellectual appreciation or an emotional sense, it was a deep recognition that my life had been of service to this singular issue that had come up in my mind so often over the years.

I saw that all my life was in one way or another directed to heal that pain and that it wasn't about *my* pain alone but about the ignorance in the world of why we are here that was reflected in every issue from education to leadership. My childhood experiences, my studies in philosophy, even my business life were, as I saw, all experiments in living conducted to find a way to ease that inner feeling of being disengaged and lost. I was becoming conscious that this was a part I played not because I had written my mission statement to that effect, but because I could recognize that my life's mission was always within the context of responding to that fundamental truth. Childhood, adolescence, and adulthood were a journey of becoming conscious of this truth.

My first act was, surprisingly, to clear out my office and clean it in a way I had never done before, with a devotion and intelligence that saw that the act was facilitating the growth of my self within the truth of my situation. I could see that action was not direct, not reactive, not pressured to sort out—it was more akin to principles that our forefathers were guided to follow when they tended the land, sowed, gave nourishment, and reaped the crops. Technology has spawned a whole new set of metaphors that have discarded the most basic principles of how we observe life working. The seasons are a model of a powerful international company that annually yields huge profits, but we tend to not think of them that way—we take them for granted.

I began to write this book five years ago—or, as many have said before, it began to write me. I chronicled my own journey of applying the seven steps. As I accomplished some measure of success at each step, I was able to write it down and use my learning in various fields to substantiate it. My "action man" identity would rear its head from time to time, urging me to form a company, share this knowledge with others—but I didn't. I just kept tending to the process, nourishing it, and waiting to see the first spring.

As I became firmly centered in a new realm of intelligence, something very interesting happened. I was contacted by a company I had worked with some years before and invited to speak at a conference.

Having seen that my mission had nothing to do with founding some future company or success, it was about being open and growing in a new state of affairs that was quite unlimited, I was beginning to feel comfortable and safe with the unknown. When I was invited to speak at this conference I saw that this was an inevitable next step in the sequence of this journey.

The conference was on the subject of stress and the audience largely consisted of doctors and practitioners in the health sector. My turn to speak came on the third day. I had by then heard international experts in all branches of medicine deliver fine and excellent speeches on the subject of stress, its implications for the nervous system, current drugs available, new brain science findings, and so on.

As I sat there, I realized that at any moment I was going to be invited to speak and I saw myself as I had done on my veranda. I am not a medical expert. I had considered medical school but had taken up philosophy for no apparently conscious reason. I felt a bit of an impostor at this conference. I also felt how much this feeling of being an impostor mattered to me and had always mattered. How many times can we honestly feel we are really in a position to be the expert in a situation? Do we not select situations in which we are not too challenged for precisely that reason—the fear of being found out? This sets almost immovable limitations on ourselves.

I had always felt either superior or inferior to the circumstances I found myself in. When inferior I was careful to cultivate a slightly humble demeanor and when superior I could run at full throttle—but neither was real. Both acts were born out of an act of self-judgment. In this situation I saw that my conception of expertise was identity based and had been for most of my life. Was my own unique journey of becoming not its own authority, if I had conducted that journey intelligently and honestly?

I quietly folded up my notes and knew without a shadow of doubt that no harm could come to me if I was myself and I knew *why*. I was a hostage walking free.

"I would like to introduce Richard..." The words surprised me after all the time I had been sat there projecting myself, my speech, and the reception I hoped to get. I had been so absorbed in my own process. I realized that there had been hardly a laugh or a joke for three days and that rather than there being any ease and wellbeing, the room was full of stress.

I began in the most unlikely place, chatting on until I felt people were engaged. I was deeply settled that it was what I was becoming that was the most unique contribution I could make to this conference and not some information I would present. It was being at ease with the unknown that was the intelligence that the situation required. I don't think I mentioned the subject of stress once, but I do know I was able to relieve stress in every person in that room during the next couple of hours and, most importantly in my own journey, served to release a small but significant intelligence of why we are here.

I relate this story to say honestly and openly that if I have become more intelligent through this journey it is not because I have studied brain science or philosophy or business. It is because I feel engaged in the unlimited realms of becoming and this has enabled me to know why I act the way I do.

A series of journeys

The notion of knowing ourselves by a series of journeys is a consistent theme in psychology, philosophy, religion, and mythology. Life is a journey of coming back to where things began and seeing what we did not have the consciousness to see at first, that we now can see as if for the first time. One could say that we are born with a purpose but only by becoming separate from it can we fulfill life's first purpose, which is to discover the purpose of life. Only then can we consciously and deliberately live it.

It is a feature of SQ individuals that they return again and again to the same issues and see more and more each time. Our departure from the early harmonies of SQ, EQ, and IQ is characterized by seeing things clearly in our early years, losing interest in our adolescence, and then moving on restlessly to the next experience to try to find something new.

Some religions say that the work we do not complete here we are destined to return to complete later and that we cannot elevate to the next level until we have learned the lessons at the existing level. Daily life has the same message. If I see the job I do in the same way today as yesterday, if I see people with the same expectations as I did yesterday, I will live the same day as I did yesterday: a kind of eternal "Groundhog Day." American philosopher George Santayana puts it this way: "Those who cannot remember the past are condemned to repeat it."

Mission explains why we are here

The unifying act of the brain is consciousness itself. Consciousness is a new level of self that has not arisen from experience alone, cannot be detected in brain function alone, has not been distilled from nurture and nature alone, but is a partnership of the self with an engagement in the permanent truth of the situation. It is only when we return to what was once important, what we once knew with certainty that we have lost and found again, that we become conscious.

The brain behaves as a single entity not by coordinating many functions from one central intelligence agency, but by being engaged in a larger unifying field of intelligence.

In a delightful film called *The Chosen*, two Jewish boys are growing up in New York in the years running up to the foundation of the state of Israel. One, the son of a rabbi, is educated to believe that no one can claim the Jewish state as theirs and that it is God's right alone. The other, the son of a secular Jewish scholar and Zionist, believes in the armed fight to take the state as their own.

As the story unfolds, the rabbi's son excels in his studies and seems to be dutifully following in his father's footsteps, but the father is concerned that his son does so only because of the weight of tradition and not by his own choice. The father rejects the son in order to force him to feel and choose for himself. It causes pain to both but more so to the father, in that he has chosen to distance his son and fears he will lose him for ever.

In the final scene of the film, the son is seen looking more like a secular Jew, his hair cut short, dressed in a smart suit, on his way to college. He has had to find his own path and yet it would be a shame if the childhood love the father and son shared were gone for ever.

Over this final scene, a story from the Talmud is narrated. A king has a son who has gone astray from his father.

The son was told, "Return to your father."

The son said, "I cannot."

Then his father sends a messenger to say, "Return to your father as far as you can and I will come to you the rest of the way."

This could be the story of our partnership with mission. We come as far as we can and we are assisted the rest of the way. It is our recognition of mission that allows it to become clearer and appear closer. It was always there—we were simply not in touch with the intelligence to see it.

DEENVELOPMENT EXERCISES

1   Don't yearn to have an important mission. This makes you divided. This is often prompted by the misconception that mission is to be recognized by others as being important. Mission is the fulfillment of the truth of the situation and is the light of your self shining out in doing what you were meant to do. Curiously, mission is the ultimate choice—the choice to give up choosing, to become of service to something great (always to serve a higher truth or principle and *never* to serve another person).

2   Don't wind yourself up to grandeur, find settlement in small acts of service. Recognize that the continuity from self to future is not by self-pressure but by small acts that nurture steady and continuous growth.

3   Have time to contemplate the central core subject of evolution and recognize that the trace of mission has been woven throughout world history. Make the bold step of becoming conscious of the unique contribution you have made not in making a big noise or creating a big business but in bringing new consciousness about the meaning of being alive and engaging in the opportunity to grow and evolve.

DEVELOPMENT EXERCISES

1   Recognize human greatness wherever you can and make it emphatically governing on your perceptions. If you are only recognizing mission in you, you will cut off from the truly compelling evidence that each human is born for greatness. Tell others when you recognize mission in their acts and gladly suffer the identity reaction in self that wants it for self only. Mission is not personal first—it is personal by our choice to be of service to it. We cannot choose mission, it chooses us!

2   Become interested in your childhood, not by going back sentimentally to the good old days, but by developing the sentiment that mission rescues our childhood from being abandoned by bringing it to fruition. Recollect those things that you were really caught by in your childhood and struggle to fulfill them in adulthood. Mission fulfills what is already written by recognizing that we are driven by who we are at core to become more.

3   If you want to write a mission statement, begin by acknowledging the human intelligence and genius through the ages of which each of us is a part. Your intelligence credentials are the core of your mission statement. It is not about how much you have learnt but about how successfully you have released the inner brilliance of your SQ. Mission is not about doing something at some time in the future—it is a *now* intelligence.

12

The Spiritually Intelligent Self

Real intelligence serves a process that is greater than ourselves. It is not something that we have or something that serves our own purposes only, it serves to bring life forward, it is evolution on the move—us and life growing simultaneously. SQ intelligence brings the consciousness of our purpose to mind.

The seven steps form a guide for the individual journey and they can offer a guide to understanding the challenges we face in the larger world in which we live. The SQ individual's actions and the steps they take imply how they want the world to be. This is the journey from awareness to consciousness. We are at first acutely aware of our self in our world and later come to be conscious of the meaning of our self in the larger world. There can be no difference between our walk and our talk.

Sogyal Rinpoche says in *The Tibetan Book of Living and Dying*:

> *True spirituality is to be aware that if we are interdependent with everything and everyone else, even the smallest, least significant thought, word and action has real consequences throughout the universe.*

Among the many checks and balances that the evolutionary process provides, there can be none more profound than this.

Our evolution requires us to be aware of our deeper nature and our conscious development requires that we value our deeper nature in taking our next steps. The future must bring new insights into our past and new values.

In presenting this work around the world, there is one question I am asked more than any other: "How can one person make a difference?" Most people think that just one person trying to make a change in the world or in a nation, a company, a school, or even a family is not going to make much difference. It is curious how history often bears out quite the opposite view and, again, it is the way we employ our intelligence that would lead us to see this.

Through the journey of this book, we first of all identified that the first task we face is to become reconnected to the whole of our intelligence resource, our SQ, our EQ, and our IQ. This could only be accomplished by deenveloping the assumption that we have built in the absence of our higher intelligence that we can solve problems at the level at which they were created. Solving problems is the evolutionary challenge and it is our SQ, our ever-evolving intelligence, that best faces the challenge.

Then, as we deenvelop the identity of self, we tune into our higher SQ intelligence resources through the triune of understanding—awareness, meaning, and evaluation—to become centered in the truth of our situation.

From a centered place in self we can act with clear vision, projection, and the recognition that our actions are "meant to be," they are the naturally evolving next steps, they are a mission.

The seven steps enclose a threefold process of understanding the truth of our situation (Steps 1, 2, 3), being centered in the truth of our situation (Step 4), and then acting based on the truth (Steps 5, 6, 7) in the larger world.

All SQ individuals who act from an SQ core, who know why they do what they do, are always acting from the same mission: to bring new levels of intelligence into the world.

We tend to view intelligence from our disconnected level of self, looking in to an inner vacancy (Figure 13). We then try to fill that inner vacancy with an identity, be it as a leader, a doctor, a teacher, a business person, or whatever, so that we do not feel alone or isolated. We regard intelligence as something that fills that inner space and covers the inner feeling of being lost, and we classify everything accordingly. Worse still, we classify others in the same way, beginning with our children. By so doing, we lock ourselves out from the potential of our SQ core and the new levels of intelligence we are yet to evolve to.

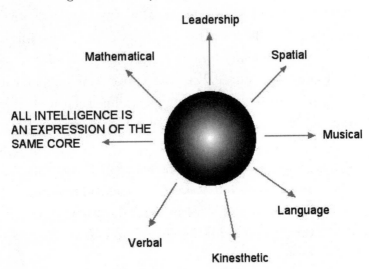

Figure 13 We view intelligence from the disconnected self

We tend to think of someone "having" intelligence, which is applicable to the mental abilities we associate with IQ, rather than being able to find the intelligence that applies to the truth of the situation as it truly is.

Filling ourselves up with intelligence of this kind can be detrimental to the greater potential of our life. I have met many people who are deemed to be highly intelligent and successful but who, in private moments, tell me: "I wish I had become a concert pianist or a writer, rather than running a big company. That is what I really wanted to do."

Such people are often driven by background and family expectations to make career choices early and to find their niche. While this is inevitable and many of the great SQ individuals were similarly driven by outside influences, their greater intelligence potential could still appear as a crisis in which the core of self is resurrected.

Figure 14 Intelligence is an expression of liberation and wholeness

The expressions of human genius from core are endless and multiple (Figure 14). If we were less willing to judge intelligence on a scale of 1 to 10, awarding points for abilities, learnt or inherited, and more willing to acknowledge the journey of life in becoming, we would be more able to acknowledge human brilliance in all walks of life. Our expressions may be very, very different, but our core reason for living is the same.

SQ is essentially a coactive, cooperative, cohesive intelligence. All those who seek to engage with all they may become add their weight to its increase in the world. If it were possible to measure such intelligence and say that Shakespeare or da Vinci, Gandhi or Mother Teresa might release 500 units of this higher intelligence, whereas another person, you or me, might release 100 units, it would not change the core importance, that the mission of all serves the same ends.

We make our assessment of intelligence from the wrong place, looking inward to a space we hope to occupy rather than outward from our own expression of a new level of self. From the self-chosen, self-found core, spiritual intelligence wishes only to serve, to expand, to be active in the human experience by bringing new intelligence into the world.

What does it mean to be spiritually intelligent?

We haven't yet devised an SQ intelligence test and I hope we never do. SQ is not a "top of the class" kind of intelligence. What we can detect are signs and symptoms of an SQ life in becoming. In this everyone can win. I am often asked whether this or that person is SQ and sometimes whether I am SQ, but it is better to ask what are the SQ processes we can recognize.

The following seven levels of the evolving SQ self can be recognized as trends of becoming. It is only possible to give a few examples at each of the seven levels. The point is to show how all-pervading SQ is and how all SQ intelligence contributes to the line of human evolution from adolescence to adulthood. It serves a purpose that is greater than merely having some intelligence. SQ does not regard one level as lesser than another but all as working toward a unified and integrating purpose.

Awareness makers

❖ Musicians, poets, writers, artists (Shakespeare, Mozart, Beethoven, and countless others) who have made us aware through their arts of our deeper feelings that have significance in the phases of intelligent life.

❖ Sportspeople who remind us of the grace and beauty of the human body and how it is more than a mere machine (athletes, skiers, gymnasts…), who have chosen to express their urge to do in the form of excellence, and who celebrate the uniqueness of the human effort and struggle.

Meaning bringers

❖ Moral individuals who have clarified the consequences of actions that are ill thought out, scientists who have sought to clarify what is ethical or not to explore and to view their work within a larger context than social pressure or ego gain.

❖ Generals and individual soldiers who have sought not to react under pressure and foolishness, whose uncertainty was constructive uncertainty.

❖ Teachers who have overcome their inhibitions to be of good service to others, and nurses and doctors who have drawn strength from wanting the best for others.

Evaluators

❖   People who in facing challenging issues, whether large or small, have looked afresh to avoid assumptions and therefore realized that there was more to find, more to do, and more to explore.

❖   Those who challenged their own and their culture's assumptions and discovered new cures, new solutions to old problems, new ways to teach children to improve relationships and to overcome life's challenges from an elevated level of self.

Centerers

❖   Individuals whose life story centers us. Those who have endured extreme crisis and yet have continued to find value in life.

❖   People such as Viktor Frankl who, having lived through the horror of Auschwitz, continued to forgive and demonstrate compassion, and the countless others like him all over the world who have not allowed terrible experiences to be an excuse not to try afresh.

❖   All who have lost friends or loved ones and continued to resist bitterness and blame and sought to overcome their emotions to find new meaning.

❖   Those who have been centered enough to forgive ignorance and choose to educate and bring light—people such as Kofi Annan, Abraham Lincoln, and Nelson Mandela.

❖   Those who have died with dignity and been able to face themselves with self-value.

Visionaries

❖ Those who see that in daily events there is always more to be done and to win. The cleaner who gets the school ready because she wants the children to have the best opportunity to grow; the father or mother who perceives the natural inner light in their children and seeks every opportunity to see that light released.

❖ The business leader who refuses to be governed by petty advantage taking and the cynicism that suggests nothing can be done and who will work for a higher good.

❖ Storytellers who reveal the true nature of the human character, those who try to heal the mind and release others rather than always trying to exercise their remedies on others.

❖ Those who take up a profession with extraordinary devotion because they want to see something worthwhile happen, not from personal advantage or fame.

Projectors

❖ Those who try to bring new intelligence to each and every situation, be it through a joke, a look, a refusal to criticize and suppress, who give of themselves freely, not to win favor or position but because they want and believe that only good can come from good whether they are associated with it or not.

❖ Those great minds that can hold a picture of a future and live with the adversity and unpopularity that the exercise of it brings.

❖ Those whose presence brings relief from suffering, the Dalai Lama, Mother Teresa, Florence Nightingale—and the person on the street who champions the same line of intelligent growth.

Missionaries

❖ Those who integrate a universal issue with a personal cause: Gandhi, Nelson Mandela, Mother Teresa, Albert Schweitzer, and countless others who are part of a team in which they have played the mission part.

Remember that these are all parts of the greater human team— they work in their own way toward one integrated mission. We are intelligent because of the part we play in something greater than ourselves. Perhaps you and I in our small but significant way can add our weight to the mission of these times as it finds a new level—whatever our style and territory of expression.

Index

Dedication

This book would quite simply not have been possible without my personal acquaintance of Leo Armin and my knowledge of his work. His philosophical writings are a true template by which to understand our human situation and I wholeheartedly dedicate this book to him.

I first met Leo in 1975. I was by then in my mid-20s and the connective tissue of meaning that was intimately intertwined through my childhood years had long since unraveled. My inner world of knowing had quietly shut me out and I was consigned to make my home in the outlands of that enchanted core. In the absence of any real template by which to understand my situation, I was lost and knew no way to lead my life in any original or meaningful way.

And yet, quietly and passionately, I continued to long to rejoin that inner place of meaning that adult life had encroached on. I believe that I still would be to this day, had I not met Leo.

There is no way to receive the gift of real knowledge and not feel oppressed. Oppression makes us try to extend that gift to others in the most considered and most excellent way we can. To pass on the jewels of wisdom is the duty of all generations. If this book enables others to relocate that inner and spiritual intelligence that is the meaning of who we have evolved to be, it will have been worthwhile.

My wish for this book is that it lends its weight to the obvious growing trend appearing in our world to find a new level of intelligence to solve the significant problems that we face.

Acknowledgments

The project to bring the spiritual dimension of human life to a large audience in a practical and substantive way began for me over 25 years ago. In that time so many people have influenced my life in moments and over long periods, I cannot name them all.

Among all my friends and colleagues with whom I have been fortunate enough to have been in research all these years, I want to mention Stephen Isaacs, John Hannon, and Daniel Goldenberg, who specifically helped me with the book, and John Turner, whose great insights into world theater have helped to fashion the practical side of SQ training.

My more recent associates helped me to bring such a difficult subject as the enigma of self and consciousness to a clearer and more concise form. We all found it an immense struggle to bring the realms of the unlimited to the limitations of the printed page.

In particular, I want to thank Nick Brealey, my publisher, who had the vision to see the shape of the ideas and helped to frame them more clearly; his great team including Victoria, who have helped market and promote the cause; Sally Lansdell, my editor; Hanserik Tonnheim, my agent; Eva Ljungkvist, who has liaised with business leaders to bring SQ to business; and Dr. Stephen Porges, who has profoundly influenced my understanding of the way brain science supports the spiritual dimensions of life.

Finally, my wife and best companion Joan has been my support and sanity quite literally every step of the way.

Thank you all.

Richard A. Bowell
Denmark, August 2004

SQ-training

SQ-training is a company established by the author, Richard A. Bowell.

SQ-training offers assistance to business, health, education, and the individual in developing higher intelligence solutions. It works with highly trained and skilled associates operating in Europe, the USA, and Canada.

Training choices

The Seven Steps of Spiritual Intelligence

The core insights and lessons from this book offered in a live training environment, with practical exercises and personal coaching.

Self-Leadership

Focusing on the inner resource of choice and how it applies at all moments in our life. This course is the foundation for leadership skills in all expressions of life.

The Cooperative Team

Our perception of self and others is often that we are competing for space, for recognition, for acknowledgment. The three intelligences working in harmony provide a different perspective. Our brilliance is in the expression of our mission and in our mission the team can naturally form.

Stress, a Positive Force for Change

Times of stress can be the herald of a new level of self. Pacifying the symptoms or covering up the problem can be to miss the enormous challenge and opportunity for change that stress heralds. We are all looking for a new level of intelligence to do more, be more effective, with less stress.

Communication Skills: Trusting Your Intelligence

We are all presenting ourselves all the time. Altering the manner and style is only a small part of the skill of presentation. With SQ, presentation becomes more live and spontaneous with the release of one's inner intelligent self.

The International SQ-Training Academy: Training the Trainer

Training SQ begins in self. It is not a set of formulae or quick-fix solutions that can be learnt. It is a deep, caring core that has a mission to be of service in bringing the personal and collective potential of individuals and organizations to new levels of intelligence.

SQ for the Classroom: A Children's Work Program

The inner engagement of children in learning and discovery is greatly enhanced when the educators are able to recognize the frameworks of how intelligence is influencing the daily growth of the children. The educator can use the model of the three intelligences in developing their role as educators and in recognizing the true potential of children.

To stay in touch with the development of spiritual intelligence worldwide, visit our website or send us an email and we will send you details of activities available and a newsletter about the development of SQ.

For further information about courses, workshops, presentations, and lectures, tapes, and books on "new intelligent solutions," please contact us:

Visit our website on www.sq-training.com or write to us at info@sq-training.com.

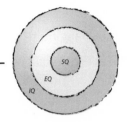

SQ-TRAINING

ACCESSING AND OPTIMISING YOUR HIGHER INTELLIGENCE

THE TRAINING

SQ-training has been working successfully with both individuals and corporate clients including international banks, management institutes, schools and educational centres, healthcare facilities, IT companies, NLP and other training organisations and has presented at leadership and management conferences around the world. The academy is headquartered in London and Denmark and SQ-training will be establishing offices in the US in 2005.

THE TEAM

In addition to Richard Bowell, the SQ-training team comprises a group of highly accomplished international trainers with credentials in psychology, stress management, life coaching, education, health & alternative therapies, meditation, theatre, presentation & communication arts, and much more.

Visit us at: www.SQ-Training.com
e-mail info: info@sq-training.com